A Day
Flip-Flops

Rita Marcotte

ISBN 978-1-63961-863-7 (paperback)
ISBN 978-1-63961-864-4 (digital)

Christian Faith Publishing
832 Park Avenue
Meadville, PA 16335
www.christianfaithpublishing.com

Printed in the United States of America

To the inspiration and catalyst of this story, my husband, Christopher.

My love and gratitude to my children, Soleil, Zachary, Samuel, and my parents, who made living the journey worthwhile.

In the Beginning

"A used-car salesman and a Catholic school teacher. I don't know," was the joke told by the best man at our wedding, followed by a smirk and a giggle of uncertainty. The guests laughed, but I think the same question was on many minds that night. Oil and vinegar perhaps is a description of how our personalities compare.

In a room, there is no ignoring Chris. Class clown, confident, and charismatic are all descriptors of Chris. He always has a joke or a story to tell, and he is very willing to share it. Me, on the other hand, the opposite. Wallflower, shy, and reserved. I am more comfortable sitting back to watch and listen to others. But as the adage says, "Opposites attract." That unequivocally describes us.

Chris, son of a well-to-do White family living in an affluent rural community. He grew up living on a quiet plat in a single-family home surrounded by woods and a white picket fence. In contrast, I was born to a blue-collar family. My upbringing consisted of the blending of two cultures, having a French-Canadian mom and a Filipino dad. Both my parents worked in order to provide for our family, scrimping and saving enough to move our family out of the tenement apartment into a single-family home in a nicer part of the city.

There isn't much that we can say is similar between the two of us. There is one thing, however, that we do have in common: It is our faith. Our belief in God, that He has a plan for us, is what brought us together and has sustained us all these years. But I get ahead of myself.

Well, I have a story to share. It's full of miraculous events. Much of what I will share, you may question or attribute to exaggeration. Other instances of my account may be a bit humdrum and boring as much of our lives can be. Rest assured that what you are about to read are true events. All the events and situations that I share with you, my family and I have truly experienced. Once you have finished reading our story, I believe that you might shake your head and ask yourself the simple questions, What are the chances? What are the odds of all those things happening to one couple? Is it fortuity, or was there a plan devised by God? A plan to test their faith? To test their determination to survive and provide a life for their family? Or were the events set in place to test their love?

However, without the grace of God, we would not be here to share our experiences. Both Chris and I started our lives with the odds against us. In 1964, Chris conceived out of wedlock, a situation frowned upon during that time. Circumstances could have turned out somewhat differently if his biological mother's family did not make arrangements for his mom. They provided her the ability to stay and give birth at a home for unwed moms. After delivery, he was put up for adoption, placed initially into foster care but officially set with his adoptive family at the age of five months.

My story began with my mom going into labor months early, giving birth to a severely underweight fragile infant. I was not provided with a luxurious birthing location, welcomed into the world with only the assistance of the police officer who responded to the emergency call. The officer quickly wrapped me in a bath towel and hurried me out of the third-floor naval-housing apartment, down the stairs, and placed me into an awaiting ambulance. Later, I remained in the hospital for over a month for treatment and observation. Obviously we were fighters, and it is our belief that God's plan for us was set right from the beginning.

So why have I written our story? We all experience difficult times in our lives that bring us to question why or feel discouraged. Anxiety, frustration, and despair can lead individuals to feel overwhelmed and be consumed by negativity. I honestly learn vicariously from others' experiences, finding guidance from stories of others that have persevered through tough times. It brings to mind the Native American proverb "Walk a Mile in His Moccasins" written by Mary T. Lathrap in 1895. Trying to live my life by the advice of this proverb has helped me to look beyond my troubles, look beyond my circumstances. Taking the view or gaining strength or reassurance from the experiences of others has been how I have persevered through difficult times in my life.

I may not wear moccasins, but my flip-flops have an interesting and encouraging tale to share. I hope you gain some insight or strength from my account to help you face adversity or when life's roller coaster drops you into one of those horrifying turns. The Lord has bestowed blessings on all of us. It's just our responsibility to find and recognize them to draw strength from during our journey.

Kismet?

Right after high school graduation, Chris actively searched for direction. Needing a source of income made it imperative that he learn a trade since attending college was not an option. His drive to support himself led to numerous construction jobs. Being young and full of energy helped during his hands-on instruction. Later in his twenties, with the financial atmosphere open to lending to budding entrepreneurs, he started his business. His skills in construction made renovating and flipping real estate financially rewarding.

By twenty-three, he was on the fast track. Working hard during the days and spending money with no worries after hours. Chris appeared to have achieved success early and was determined to make it last. People were impressed by him, driving a new SUV, living in a condo on the East Side of the city, and eating out nightly with his friends. Chris's confidence and outlook were untouchable.

But then the financial crash of the '80s happened. He lost everything. After losing his company, he was once again lost and searching for direction. Watching what he thought was the ultimate success come tumbling down like a house of cards forced him to reevaluate his priorities. He found a groundskeeper job and housing in the Hamptons with his eldest sister and her husband. Spending a couple of years in New York was just what Chris needed to figure out what direction he should take.

Rejuvenated and sun-kissed from his time in East Hampton, Chris returned to Rhode Island. Returning to his hometown was a humbling experience. He was determined to settle back down and start anew. Upon returning, he was grateful to his family once again. His other sister and brother-in-law welcomed him back and invited him into their home to help him get back on his feet. He started job searching and found employment—a job selling furniture at the local Sears and Roebuck store. It was not his dream job, but it was a job. It provided him with a paycheck and an opportunity to regain his confidence and his drive to succeed. After a couple of weeks of working there, he was ready to put, as his mother would refer to, "his gift of gab" to work.

He interviewed and obtained a job selling cars. This job suited him. He always loved cars, loved driving them, reading about them; so why not try his hand at selling them? Each day brought new experiences. He settled in selling Subarus, meeting interesting people, forming connections in the car business network, and bringing home a pay.

Eventually, he was able to find and move into an apartment of his own. The apartment was not fancy but was almost perfect for a young bachelor. Located in the center of town with restaurants, convenient stores, coffee shops, everything a single guy could need—even the tenants that lived in the compound were great. A lovely little old lady named Gertrude, who lived with her mother, resided in the apartment beside him. Like it or not, he had a motherly eye watching his comings and goings.

The apartment was perfect except for the laundry, which was located between his and Gertrude's apartments. Early morning washings, with the banging of the washing machine filled with soiled laundry created by the elderly mom, was a source of contention. One that neither of them was willing to concede to. Chris would often times walk out into the laundry half asleep in his boxer shorts, angrily waving his arms, yelling, "Can't you do that in the morning?"

Gertrude, adamantly shaking her head, would respond with, "Mom spoiled the sheets again. They have to be cleaned!" As I said, it was almost perfect.

*****

At this time, as a young adult, many things were happening in my life as well. I was starting my senior year of college, starting student teaching as an education major, and looking forward to graduation. Not only were things falling into place academically but also on a personal level. I recently became engaged to literally the boy next door. He was the neighbor's grandson. He had moved in to help his grandmother after his grandfather passed away. We started dating when I was eighteen, right after my high school graduation.

I was ready to start my life journey with my first boyfriend and love. It was wedding planning time. So my parents and I spent a day looking over reception locations. Narrowing down the choices based on previous weddings and formal dances that we all attended was the easy part. Agreeing on a venue was a different story. Eventually, we put down a deposit on a banquet hall for the wedding reception; it was ideal because it also was a hotel. Distant relatives traveling for the wedding would be able to stay right at this location in reserved rooms.

After having lunch in the hotel's restaurant, my parents mentioned that I should start searching for a new car. They felt that as an upcoming graduate and soon-to-be married woman, that I should have reliable transportation. The hall's location was on Route 44, a road dotted with many car dealerships selling both new and used vehicles. After a brief drive, we pulled into a Plymouth dealership.

Not sure why we stopped there because we had to pass the Ford dealership, which is the make that my father usually favored.

A sales manager greets us as we enter the showroom. He asks, "What brings you to the dealership today? What can I help you with?" He informs us that he will have someone join us to answer any questions and help us with our search. As we look over the cars in the showroom, we hear a salesman paged to the showroom.

After a few moments, in enters a jovial, horn-rimmed glasses-wearing salesman. He introduces himself, "Hi, I'm Chris." He shakes my father's hand, then my mother's, and then finally mine. My dad explains that we are searching for a car for my graduation. Chris enthusiastically explains how the car manufacturer has a college graduate promotion. This information sounds intriguing to my father, always looking to find the best deal. Since I was still at home, he knew deep down that he would be helping with the payment until I was out of the house.

During the extent of his sales pitch, Chris hardly looked at me, with focused attention on my father. I found myself growing angry that this salesman was going through the aspects of the car with my father. Because the car was going to be mine! The decision to buy was mine, and this chauvinist was not even looking at me.

Negotiation takes place, haggling over the last few dollars for the monthly payment, finishing with my mom demanding a set of floor mats. Eventually, we buy the car, which is a cute all-back Sundance America. It had crank windows and no air condition, which I was ready to forfeit to meet my monthly payment goal. What a mistake that was! Summer in a black car with no air was not fun! However, it was the one located in the showroom. The car was clean and ready to go.

We are asked to return the next day to sign paperwork and obtain the car. The following day ended up being a Saturday. We arrive early and excited. To our dismay, we are moved into a room to wait. Chris pops his head in after some time, which feels like a lifetime, and apologizes. He informs us that as luck would have it, that he was responsible to coordinate multiple car deliveries and that it may be a bit of a wait. Paperwork is signed, and we end up waiting again—this time, for the license plate.

Chris finally comes back, states that the license plates are not in, suggests that my parents head home, and reassures them that he will take care of the issue. Tired, my parents happily agree and head home. Eventually, Chris returns and explains that he will put dealer plates on my car and follow me home to take the plates back to the dealership. With promises that he will return on Monday with my license plates, I reluctantly agree, disappointed that I won't be able to drive my new car during the weekend.

At this point, I have been at the dealership nearly all day. To apologize, Chris asks if I would join him for a bite to eat. I decline graciously. However, he is persistent and ends the dinner offer with, "You have waited all day. Let me make it up to you. You must be hungry. It's so late in the day, and I will be eating alone." Not sure if it was my Catholic guilt, as my friend once told me I operate on, or if I was genuinely starving from my long wait; but I was persuaded to join him. It was a platonic dinner; I was hungry, and he wouldn't have to eat alone.

Okay, Sure!

Well, we ate at a local family restaurant down the street from my home. Our conversation was light; he asked about me, my education, my family. He willingly shared some stories about himself, telling me about his family, how he liked sports, and how he grew up with the owners of the restaurant that we were eating in. A tidbit of information shared, perhaps trying to impress me. He was very inquisitive; and I'm unsure why or how it never came up, but I never shared the fact that I was engaged. Why did I have to? It wasn't a date. I just had a bite to eat with the person who sold me my car; at least, that is what I was trying to convince myself.

Before leaving, Chris orders some appetizers from the restaurant. He walks me to my house and hands the appetizers to my mother. Touched by the thoughtfulness, she invites him to our family's fourth of July party the following weekend. Without hesitation, he happily accepts the invitation. As he leaves, I turn with my mouth wide open and ask, "Why did you do that? What are you thinking?"

"He will never come. He was just being polite," my mom states to reassure me. Being innocent with accepting the dinner offer, I now was feeling like I was in an episode of the comedy show *I Love Lucy*, and the words that her husband would say to her when she was in trouble were ringing through my head: *You've got some 'splaining to do, Lucy*. Well, I guess I have some explaining to do. Reflecting on the dinner's offer, conversation, and his quick acceptance to the party, I realized that I was in a situation and that things were not going to go over well with my fiancé. In my heart of hearts, I knew I didn't do anything wrong. It was a simple meal, but I know my fiancé would not agree or see it that way.

So I got right to work. My friends that were coming were given a task to keep Chris and my fiancé apart. Get through the party, and everything will be fine. Easier said than done. Chris arrived with his lifelong friend, Sal.

Everywhere I went, Chris went; he followed me like a puppy dog. I later found out that he had plans himself. He assigned Sal the task to sit back and watch the guests. "There must be a boyfriend, and we will find out tonight." So with our friends doing a great job of managing and keeping people occupied, Chris makes an announcement to everyone. In a loud voice, he exclaims, "Rita, learning how much you like baseball from our dinner the other night, please come to New York with me. I have tickets to the Red Sox and Yankee game. I will rent you your own room. No funny business. We will have the time of our lives." Yes! That's right. You can imagine that Chris was able to identify my fiancé at this point because he was the one my father was holding back. Chris left very soon after, with me having some explaining to do.

After that fateful dinner, Chris continued to pursue me. He sent flowers every other day for a few weeks. Trying to make a good impression with my family, Chris consulted a mechanic who just happened to be a Filipino. Chris followed his advice: to do some work around the house, which would earn him a meal with the family.

While I was away on a day trip with my parents and my fiancé, Chris—with his brother-in-law's help—recapped the metal trim around the front windows. It was quite impressive, and as predicted, he was asked to dinner. The evening provided my family an opportunity to introduce Chris to some traditional Filipino dishes. However, it also offered Chris a forum to share stories about himself. Sharing that he had lost his company and all his properties was a detail that my parents had not received well. Upon leaving, as we said our goodbyes, we watched as Chris approached his car. There, leaning on the car, was my fiancé.

Words were exchanged, but each of them separated peacefully—perhaps because my parents and I were nervously watching from the front door. Having an audience was the finger in the dam holding back the trouble that could have ensued. Relieved that a fight did not happen, as he drove away, my father felt obligated to share his thoughts about our guest. "You have plans to be married, you are an educated girl, and you do not know what his intentions are. He is a deadbeat. Get rid of him." Hoping that night would have been the literal and figurative closing of the door regarding Christopher.

But it wasn't. That summer, I was working for the city's recreation department as a camp counselor. One hot summer afternoon, after camp, I was surprised by Chris. There he was, leaning on my car with a quart of frozen lemonade—the only kind you could find in Rhode Island—and a packed picnic. It was evident that he wasn't giving up.

Chris conveyed his intentions and said, "If not for me, just think about what you are doing. I have been praying for you my whole life." I was faced with the hardest decision of my life. Was it his faith? His conviction that we were meant to be together? I'm not sure what it was, but I guess I believed him. I called off the wedding, and Chris and I started our courtship.

I Do!

Time went on, and I eventually graduated with my teaching degree. I was blessed to obtain a teaching position in the Catholic school that I was proud to be an alumnus of. I was the second-grade teacher. Being part of such a small-and-supportive staff was amazing. Some of the classes were taught by sisters, and others were taught by laypeople like me.

My kindergarten teacher, Sr. Ida, still lived in the convent and frequently came to the school to help out. She would look through the classroom door and smile. Later sharing with me in the teacher's room that I still look like that little kindergarten student that she had so many years ago. I treasured the time that I had to observe the sisters while they taught their students, sharing their faith, love, and patience. What exceptional mentors they were to me. During this time, I also started to build a friendship with the third-grade teacher. Nancy was a young lay teacher; it was nice to have someone to collaborate and work with that was around my age.

On Halloween night, the school was holding a costume party for the students and staff. Chris and I attended as convicts dressed in black-and-white striped costumes. The sense of community and family was evident during the evening's festivities. The pastor who was the head of the school took such joy in watching the singing and dancing, exclaiming, "Oh, entertainment." Following the Halloween party, we decided to visit Chris's sister, family, and friends.

After our visit, we had dinner. He was unusually quiet, which I attributed to being tired because it was a long evening. However, later that night, I found out why he was so quiet. He wasn't tired; he was nervous. On bended knee, he proposed to me. Dressed appropriately, I agreed to be wed and be the proverbial ball and chain.

Nov. 1, 1992
Engagement Announced

We were engaged on October 31st and announced our engagement to our families on November 1st. Soon after our announcement, we set a date for May 29, 1993. Vacation time as a teacher is frowned upon. Teacher vacations and time off are reserved for the summertime and holidays. So I suggested the date because it was Memorial Day, which meant we could celebrate our anniversary on the long holiday weekend. It would also help Chris to remember when our anniversary would be approaching; having a little reminder each year would be a good thing, so Chris agreed to the date.

So we had six months to plan, book, and schedule our wedding. Everything went relatively smoothly. My mom, mother-in-law, and I went to the local wedding and prom dress store. It was amazing; all three of us were able to find dresses on our very first visit. Chris and I chose our attendants. I asked Nancy to be one of my bridesmaids. She accepted, and I was so excited to have someone to talk to and share my wedding plans with at work each day. My first year as a teacher flew by. Spring arrived, and the wedding was approaching quickly. The school's principal and pastor were gracious to grant me a week off following the wedding.

It was time to pay the next installment for the banquet hall. We had not yet combined our banking and finances, so we withdrew money, thousands from each of our accounts, to give to the Country Club one day. Prior to making the payment, we decided to have lunch at the local D'Angelos.

With all the excitement, I left my purse at the sandwich shop. Everything we had was in the purse! Chris was furious. "How could you do that? How irresponsible! I don't know if I can marry someone that is that irresponsible." I had nothing to say. It was irresponsible. So we drove back to the sandwich shop to see if it was still there. I ran to the booth, and it was not there. My heart sank. It was hard to breathe, and the girl at the counter came walking over to me.

I didn't quite hear her at first. Tears blurred my eyes, but to my relief, she showed me my purse. "I found this after you left. Isn't this yours?" I can't recall how I thanked her, whether I hugged her or shook her hand, but she was a godsend. I do remember holding my breath as I unzipped the purse to see if the money was still there. It was! Thank God! Chris was still furious, driving in silence until we got to our destination. The ride gave him some time to cool off and regroup. We made our payment and continued with the wedding plans.

*****

Our wedding day came. My mom; Chris's sister, my matron of honor; and I went to have our hair done. It was a nice escape because my little house was bustling with all the preparations, complicated because my Filipino relatives from Colorado came to prepare for the day as well. The hustle and bustle of a little house with so many people was stressful. Once we returned from our hair appointment, waiting for the photographer, I decided to go to the mall for cinnamon buns for everyone to snack on, and then I went to the pharmacy to pick up last-minute toiletries. Unfortunately, the weather was not looking promising, with an ominous, cloudy, gray sky and a drizzle threatening with showers.

As I waited in line, there was this burly tattooed biker clad in his leather riding outfit checking out in front of me. He strikes up a conversation with the sales clerk. "It looks like it's going to be a miserable day." I don't know what came over me, but I blurt out, "Oh no, I hope not. I'm getting married today." This total stranger turns around, towering over me like a giant, and puts his hand on my shoulder and looks down at me with such a sweet and caring expression. "Oh, I'm sure it's going to be wonderful, honey. Don't worry." And he was right. The sky cleared up, and the day was beautiful.

I couldn't have dreamed of a better day. Everything ran smoothly. The limousine ride seemed like we were in slow motion, but it was my first time in one, so I savored every moment. Eventually, we finally arrived at the church. As the wedding party gathered and prepared for our entrance, the music started. The guests quietly found their seat as the beautiful music floated across the church.

Chris's niece played the flute, the organist was a bridesmaid's sister, and we even hired the music teacher from the school to play the violin. The flower girl and the ring bearer walked down the aisle to Disney's theme song, "Wish upon a Star." Finally, the "Bridal March" started.

My dad and I prepared to walk down the aisle on the white carpet that was crookedly set down by two of the groomsmen. Trying to calm my nerves, I looked down at my flower bouquet and took a deep breath, just as I used to do to calm my nerves as I would step onto the pitcher's mound during my baseball and softball years.

My flowers were gorgeous! To my mother's dismay, I was adamant to have yellow roses added to the flowers. In her opinion, the bouquet should be completely white; but ever since watching the royal wedding of Prince Charles and Princess Diana as a little girl, I was taken by her bouquet's beauty. My flowers were just as spectacular, and our wedding was just as special and magical as that royal ceremony.

We started our walk down the aisle; I could feel my dad give me a little tug, and he whispered, "Take your time." I think it was his way to savor the moment as well. Chris stood by the altar with an expression of surprise and awe. Abiding by tradition, it was the first time that he had seen my gown or seen me that day for that matter.

Chris's excitement was evident; he was like a little boy in a candy store. He kept looking over at me and talking during the mass, which is a no-no during a Catholic mass—let alone that he was in front for all to see. I guess I wasn't too mad and just kept widening my eyes, trying to signal him to be quiet. The readings were read, the ceremony and blessings performed, and then it was over with the statement of "You may kiss the bride."

As we turned to look at each other, Chris gently cupped his hands around my face, and we kissed. You could hear the gasps of astonishment from the right-hand side of the church.

The front aisles on that side of the church were reserved for my students. Watching their teacher kiss someone was utterly disgusting. Chris and I walked arm in arm down the aisle as Mr. and Mrs. Christopher Marcotte. As we reached the landing outside of the church, some of my students were there, giggling and calling out, "Hi, Mrs. Marcotte." Having my students there, hearing their giggles, and seeing their smiles touched my teacher's heart and still to this day makes me smile.

You've Got to Be Kidding

Earlier, during our wedding preparation, we started to look for a home to start our life together. One afternoon, he drives me past this run-down cottage. The cedar trees that have grown over and on it dwarfed the dwelling. No one has been living in it for a while. I started laughing and said, "Oh, look at that poor place!" You could hardly see the actual house.

Chris looks over at me and says, "Don't laugh. I just bought it." He got out and introduced me to the owners, Mr. and Mrs. Meadows, who lived right next door. What lovely people they were! Mr. Meadows had grown up in the house and built his home next door for him and his wife. Chris had found it and made an offer. We were able to close on the house a week before we were married.

So we started work on renovating the cottage. We stripped the house down to the studs. One day after work, I came home from school to find that the front of my house was completely off the structure and in the front yard. Mr. Meadows was sitting next door with his oxygen mask, laughing and gasping in the oxygen and murmuring, "Open house at the Marcottes!" I am then informed of the circumstances that had transpired earlier that day. I am horrified to hear how Mr. Meadows watched Chris cut the roof with a chainsaw in sections while he was standing on it. He shared with me that Chris fell through with the chainsaw running, and each of the other sections slapped shut like a deck of cards. And then the front of the house fell forward and off the house. Poor Mr. Meadows stood in amazement and fear as he watched the house fall around Chris, who fell straight down onto his feet with a chainsaw running. Chris's guardian angel was working overtime that day.

A welcome break came in the form of a wedding invitation. We were invited to a family member's wedding in Kennebunkport, Maine. It was nice to dress up and put aside the toolbelt. It was a glorious summer day. We enjoyed the car ride up; I was in awe as we drove up to the family homestead. The majestic house was located on a peninsula, having to drive across a tiny bridge to get to the property.

I jokingly look over at Chris and state, "Wow, I think I married into the wrong part of your family." We follow a caravan of cars to the chapel. The bride and her father proudly drove down Kennebunkport's roads in the family's '55 convertible T-Bird. The wedding was beautiful. At times, I caught the glances of wedding guests, attributing their looks to having my fancy updo (thanks to my friend's help) and being dressed in a pretty beige flowing long dress. It didn't faze me because Chris and I were not familiar family members and were not locals. However, the reason for the glances became clear to me later when we returned to the reception.

After locating our seats in the fancy outdoor tent, we found ourselves at the bar. Chris and I sat on the stone wall, drinking our cocktails and looking at the Atlantic Ocean surf. It was like a scene in a movie, watching the children run around the lush green lawn. The boys dressed in their pastel outfits and their boat shoes, teasing and taunting the little girls in their white linen dresses and their Mary

Janes, while their parents stood in the summer sun, chatting with their champagne glasses in hand.

A distant family member approached Chris and me. He curiously asks Chris about his family and extended family members. Not familiar with the details of where many extended family members resided, Chris referred to me for clarification. I notice that this individual has edged closer to Chris and had turned his back toward me with each question. He never looked at me or responded to anything I said. When there was a lull, Chris would restate what I shared, and then the conversation resumed. It was like I was invisible and he could not hear a single word I uttered. As he spoke with Chris, it was apparent that he had no interest in me and rudely had signaled me out of the conversation.

I politely removed myself and gladly obtained another beverage from the bar. It became blatantly apparent that my darker skin set me apart from the family and was the reason for the glances earlier at the chapel. I was reassured and comforted when I noticed that Chris was following me as I made my way to our table, whispering to me that that person certainly was an ignorant jackass. "Please don't let that bother you. You are the smartest, most beautiful girl here! No one can hold a candle to you."

Relieved to see that not all the family was like that other individual. The bride's father did not display any discriminatory behavior; he greeted and welcomed us by giving Chris and me a tour of his magnificent home. During dinner, we sat with others who were friends of the groom. They were not cut from the same prejudicial cloth as some of the bride's relatives and were a gregarious, sociable bunch. The conversation was light, and the food was delicious.

As the sunset and the evening passed, it was time to leave. It was a spectacular, elegant event, nonetheless tainted by my personal hurt. Saddened of being conscious and aware of being judged because of my color. My education, my accomplishments, my faith—everything about me simply dismissed. It was an experience that I have never forgotten and never will.

We worked together to finish the house. I learned how to snap lines on the roof for shingles, put up sheetrock and tile floors. When we put up the vinyl siding and I stenciled the rooms, it finally felt like home. For our first anniversary, we dug out the backyard and put in a brick patio. It was an adorable cottage, with a princess pink door, nestled in a quiet neighborhood on a dirt road. Or at least, that is what we thought until one morning.

As Chris was walking the dog in the early morning before work, a car came speeding like it was right out of a scene from *The Dukes of Hazzard*. Chris was able to dodge the car, but the newspaper delivery driver, unable to stop, hit Keeno. Keeno was the Akita puppy that Chris gave to me as a wedding present. After rushing him to a twenty-four-hour clinic and committing to two-thousand-dollars' worth of medical treatment trying to save him, we were told there was nothing that could be done. It was devastating. The anger and hurt that I felt overwhelmed me.

By this time, I had given my resignation at the Catholic school. I had been interviewing for a job in a public school in hopes of obtaining a better-paying teacher's position during the summer following our wedding.

Disappointed that I was not offered a classroom position, I reluctantly accepted a job as a teacher's aide. So I went in later the morning of the incident with red eyes and looking rather ragged from the horrifying morning.

As I settled in with my small group of students, I realized that the school's principal had decided to visit and observe my lesson. At the end of the lesson, feeling a bit self-conscious about my performance, I attempted to get feedback. I wanted her to be aware of my early morning trauma, and as I shared my story, she just gave me a comforting smile, reassured me that the lesson was fine, and asked me to visit her office later on that day.

My mind was in a whirlwind. I thought I was fired. *Why does she want to talk to me?* I gathered up the courage and went to her office. To my surprise, she shared her observations and proceeded to offer me a teaching position. There was an available position due to a teacher having difficulty and not remaining employed by the school. Who would have thought that I would be observed and offered a teaching position on such a sad, trying day?

That first year certainly was a year to remember full of heartbreak and elation. The beginning of my "training" in dealing with mishaps. We remained in that quaint little cottage for nearly three years. Being promoted to the used-car manager, Chris was doing well in the car business, and our finances were stable. It was time to move on. Time for a bigger house, and time to start a family. We optimistically and naively thought that good times were on our way. Little did we know what was ahead of us.

Next!

In 1996, we started our search for our next home. Every weekend, we would drive around the nearby rural community that we had decided would be where we would buy our forever home. Having grown up in the city, I relished the prospect of owning a house in the country with a big private yard. We were fortunate to find a property in that country community. It was a lovely gray, cape-cod style house with a long driveway that ended in a circle, bringing guests to the front of the house. The property was secluded and was just what we were looking for. However, the interior needed work, so once again, we strapped on our tool belts and started the renovations.

We hired some contractors to do the larger projects, but we continued to work on smaller projects during the weekends. That fall, we proudly announced that we were expecting our first child. So we started changing the second floor's layout. We knocked down some walls, renovated the upstairs bathroom, plastered, and painted. During the renovation we started to paint and create a nursery for our new baby-to-be. Christopher shared that he enjoyed the stories of Winnie the Pooh. Since we decided not to find out whether we were having a boy or a girl, we agreed on a Winnie-the-Pooh theme. I sketched out and painted a scene of the Hundred Acre Wood scene in the baby's room.

Thanksgiving was our first official holiday in our new home. We invited the whole family. In celebration of the new house, my parents gave us their dining room furniture to complete our celebration. Family, festive decorations, good food, and a warm, comforting fire in the fireplace made for a memorable night. Sharing baby plans while relaxing together was like a picture from a storybook. It was perfect.

Chris's mom was battling cancer and was not feeling well, but we were thankful to have her there during the holiday. The baby's birth was getting closer, and it was looking like she would be there to welcome her grandchild into this world. After spending the holiday with our family, we went to bed with grateful hearts.

That is, until about 2:00 a.m. the next morning. I awoke to a slight noise. I got up, still a bit drowsy, and walked around the house, trying to identify it. Finally, I went to the stairwell leading upstairs. The renovations were not complete, and being pregnant, we were sleeping in the guest bedroom on the first floor to stay away from the paint fumes. I quickly realized that the hum was the smoke detector going off on the second floor. There was a fire!

The smoke detectors were battery-powered at that time and not hard-wired, so none of the first-floor alarms went off. Chris was sound asleep, resting off the previous night's festive libations. I woke him up, and he went upstairs to check. He was unable to locate where the smoke was originating. It appeared that it was coming from an alcove.

As he directed me to call 911, he returned to the second floor with a fire extinguisher from the kitchen and sprayed it into the small attic. Still not completely awake, I picked up the phone. I waited for it to connect, and then I heard the message, "Information. How can I help you?" What... I dialed 411. Information? I quickly hung up and took a deep breath. I gathered myself and finally contacted 911. I informed the dispatcher that the smoke detectors were ringing and that Chris was trying to determine why. The dispatcher directed me to get out of the house immediately. I frantically called Chris to get out.

So many things were going through my mind. The renovations, the house—what do we do now? I grabbed our wedding album; our new puppy, Dakota; and evacuated as directed. Cold, crying, and confused, not sure what was happening. Pregnant and unable to do anything, wondering where Chris was. Was he okay? Where were the firefighters?

Finally, Chris came out. The volunteer firefighters arrived and entered the house. At this point, the neighbors were curiously gathering outside to see what was happening. I was rushed into an ambulance to warm up. The door was left open, and I could see the smoke billowing out of the house. I overheard some of the firefighters talking. "Someone was watching over these people."

The chief was able to locate the spot where the fire started. He ran in and cut a hole halfway down the cellar stairs and directed the others to spray in there. It was a center chimney cape, and as luck would have it for us, just the week before, they had lost the same kind of house to the same sort of fire. The fire went straight up the chimney and overtook that house, leaving it in ashes. The fire may have destroyed all our renovations, but at least our house was still standing. We would have to begin again. Once again, our guardian angels were working hard!

April Fools!

The cleanup from the fire and renovations continued. The arrival of the baby was approaching quickly. The contractor that was hired to do the roof was in the process of installing the trusses. After some time, we realized that we had fallen victim to everyone's nightmare: the disappearing contractor. How could someone leave a roof open and exposed to the winter elements of New England, knowing that the family that they were working for had a baby on the way? Thankfully, Chris was able to find a friend that was in the contracting business. After some persuading, even though most contractors frown on taking over a job started by someone else, he agreed to help us out.

In February, the family experienced a devastating loss. Chris's mom's battle with cancer ended. She bravely fought the battle and was prepared to receive her reward in heaven. I stood at her bedside, eight months pregnant. She took my hand and said a blessing over the grandchild that she would never see, never have a chance to hold. She thanked me for all I have done and for bringing out the best in her son. She was happy that he had found someone to love and cherish. It was all very overwhelming!

I tried to take a moment to regroup myself, but she wouldn't let go of my hand. Our conversation ended with, "Never forget that you are his rock. You are the rock of the family, and I know you are able. The Lord has made you a strong woman and will strengthen you and be with you whenever you ask Him. Never forget it!" I promised that I wouldn't forget. It was like she was passing the baton to me. She was always a strong, spiritual support for Chris. Such big shoes left behind, never able to be filled. Nevertheless, I continue every day trying my best to fulfill my promise to her.

Unexpectedly, April 1st brought a blizzard. As the snow accumulated, trees fell, we lost electricity, and the temperature in the house slowly started to dip. After the fire, we decided to eliminate the fireplace. We retained the fireplace for simple aesthetics; however, it was not working any longer and didn't provide any warmth. Business at the dealership was going well, so Chris thoughtfully picked out and bought a new full-size SUV. He would claim it was for the baby's protection, but I think he enjoyed the prestige that came along with driving such a luxurious vehicle.

Thankful to have it available to us now, Chris, Dakota, and I climbed into it and started our drive to my parent's home. It was not a long drive typically, but the storm had created hazardous driving conditions. Electrical wires, fallen tree branches, and poor visibility made for a very dangerous drive. As we approached the driveway, I felt at peace. It was comforting to be back at my childhood home. I took a deep sigh of relief, appreciating having heat and electricity and not to mention having my mom nearby. However, Dakota ended up being sick, vomiting and panting. Dog lovers can be adamant that dogs can sense things about their owners. As I sat on the kitchen floor comforting him, perhaps Dakota's ailments indicated upcoming events. Labor!

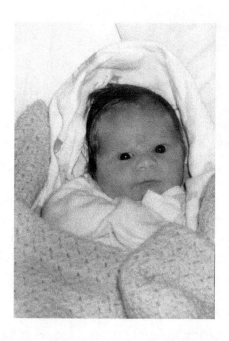

The next day involved blizzard cleanup. The contractors came to continue working on the upstairs. With the banging of hammers and the zing of the drills, we prepared to go to an appointment. Chris informed the workers that we should be home in a couple of hours. Well, we never returned that day. Eighteen hours of labor in the hospital led to an unexpected cesarean section.

Finally, on April 3, our baby girl arrived. It was time to announce her name to our family and the world. Inspiration for her name came from many places. Saddened that Chris's mom was not able to hold and see her granddaughter, we incorporated her maiden name into our daughter's name. We named her Soleil Christina. Soleil, the French word for *sun*, was fitting for our little ray of sunshine. I have never experienced the connection and love I felt as I held my blonde, curly-haired, fair-skinned baby. Her blue eyes wide open, looking back at me—what a joyous day!

Aloha!

Things were going well; with some changes to expenses, I was able to request a year-long maternity leave to care for Baby Soleil. I enjoyed my time at home with her. Time went by quickly! Since I was not working, Chris surprised me with a cruise to Hawaii. It was a trip of a lifetime. Only offered in the fall, the cruise was impossible to consider because I was a teacher. However, since I was on maternity leave, it was finally possible. He opted out of the insurance because we were determined to go, and it was expensive.

Before I knew it, Soleil was three months old. It was my mother's birthday celebration, and we decided to take the family to a popular steak restaurant. What a lovely dinner. My dad walked Soleil around, and the two of them were like celebrities. She was adorable; a friend once remarked that she resembled a cabbage patch doll with squeezable cheeks. It was nice to relax and have a peaceful meal.

Returning home, I put the baby down to nap in the upstairs nursery. I went back downstairs and started to prepare a bottle. I looked out the kitchen window and was unable to process what was going on. Chris was at the entrance of the driveway, which was over a hundred feet away, so I couldn't quite see what was going on clearly. My mind was flooded with questions, trying to make sense of what I was seeing. Was he lying down? Was he playing with Caesar, the neighbor's dog?

I went out to the front of the house to see what all of the commotion was about. I noticed that Chris wasn't sitting down; Caesar was attacking him. Suddenly, I heard him screaming, "Help, help me!" All I could think of was our dog. I turned, and my saunter turned into a sprint as the gravity of the situation finally started to hit me. I ran to Dakota—the puppy that I had protectively held in my arms during the Thanksgiving fire, now a strong, protective eleven-month-old adolescent. I swung open the glass door, and out ran the dog.

Dakota launched himself off the stairs and rocketed toward the dog. Chris was trying to hold the dog's collar and push the dog off of his leg. Unfortunately, this once docile pet had succumbed to its internal wild instincts. Being a Rottweiler, he clamped his jaws onto Chris's calf and was not letting go. Dakota plowed into the dog like a battering ram, tossing him like a ragdoll. Our dog pounced on the aggressor and, with his massive jaws, held the Rottie in place. Dakota held Caesar down and restrained him. It was like he must have pinched a nerve because Caesar didn't move a muscle.

I was running to assist Chris, and I could feel the blood drain from my face. He was gripping his leg at what looked like a red knee-high sock. As I approached, it became clear that it was not a sock; his leg was covered in blood, ripped open. I screamed to my father to call 911 as I got closer to Chris. The next-door neighbor, who was in her pool with her children, heard my screams. She jumped over the split rail wooden fence that separated our two yards. Her medical training kicking in; she frantically grabbed the beach towels strewn across the fence to use as a tourniquet. She was a nurse and quickly took charge and directed everyone's actions. I knelt next to Chris as she was wrapping his leg with the towels.

The blood kept pumping and spraying. Our neighbor took my hand and ordered me to press near his groin to slow down the blood's flow. I could hear her talking to Chris. She was saying things like, "Chris, can you hear me? Stay with us, Chris. Look at me." Her voice was like a faint murmur, like in a movie when the volume is lowered to create tension and draw attention to the main event. However, this wasn't a movie; I was once again helpless like I was during the house fire, just staring into his eyes and whispering, "You are going to be all right. You are going to be all right."

*****

32

Thank God he was. Chris had to take some time to recover; at least a couple of months out of work was the doctor's prediction. This period in our lives was stressful because it was not a given that he would be granted time off from work, and with me on maternity leave, what would we do without his pay? His employer was known as a hardened businessman. Once again, the Lord provided! His boss allowed him to take the time out and continued to pay him his weekly salary.

He recovered and returned to work before the end of summer. September arrived. Unfortunately, since Chris took so much time off to recover, he needed to work. Our vacation of a lifetime to Hawaii was no longer possible. He couldn't take vacation time, and since we thought that nothing was going to interfere with our plans, Chris did not purchase the insurance for it. We lost the trip, all the money, and the opportunity to visit the islands. It was difficult to know how to feel. Grateful that Chris made it through okay—that we made it out of a financially pressing period. But at the same time, having to grin and bear the disappointment of losing our Hawaiian cruise.

It was strange not setting up my classroom and not reporting to work in the fall. On my sister-in-law's birthday, I received a present of my own. I found out that we were expecting again. It was incredible how quickly that year passed. Christopher was working hard at the dealership. He worked so many hours. He would be called into work on his day off and out of the house early, and coming back home late was a problematic transition being home with Soleil and dealing with a second pregnancy. Chris did continue to work on projects, but they were long and drawn out. One project involved putting up doors in our bedroom that led to a mini loft overlooking our family room. I was downstairs fixing dinner. I could hear the banging and drilling. Deciding to make the doorway a nonstandard size, Chris was convinced that he could customize a door himself instead of ordering one to fit.

As I called up to him to come to dinner, he responded with an affirmative and tried to force the doorframe into the opening. As he pushed with the chisel to shave a section off, I heard him yell out the beginning of an expletive, and then silence. I have found that silence is not golden in my house. I ran upstairs and found Chris looking for gauze with one of his thumbs in his mouth. He had slipped off of the door and pierced his thumb to the point that my newly finished bedroom ceiling and walls had blood splatter like a crime scene all over it. I helped him wrap the hand, and I found myself yelling, "Watch out! Not the new rug!"

In retrospect, it was not very empathetic of me, but I just couldn't deal with cleaning, fixing, or replacing something new again. The bleeding did not stop, and it was apparent that the laceration needed stitches. Being familiar with the long wait of an emergency room visit and being pregnant with our second child, I wasn't up to packing everything we would need for Soleil. Fortunately, we had become friendly with our plumber who also lived in town. Gratefully, he answered the phone and willingly agreed to bring Chris to the emergency room.

Just Breathe

The rest of the year went by as smoothly as could be expected. Soleil was walking before she was one. Always wanting to be entertained, she was a handful. The baby was due around my mother's birthday on July 11th. As the sales manager, Chris's enthusiasm and drive benefited both the car dealership and our family. Sales went up drastically, and Chris was bringing home substantial paychecks. Unfortunately, the late nights and the pressure of having to perform and support his growing family mounted. Chris started to drink more and more. Threatening him that I would take the babies and leave forced him to promise that he would change. Making promises that he would stop drinking, and that he would be more present with me when he was home.

Unfortunately, what he was able to say was not what he was able to do. One evening, when I was at my parents' house, I called him to let him know that I would be home soon. I could tell by the tone of his voice that something was not quite right. I left Soleil with my parents under the guise that I had an errand to do. I arrived home to find Chris drunk; he just returned home from some time with his friend that he had hired to work with him at the dealership. Watching him stumble trying to stop me, slurring his apologies, broken promises to remain sober during my pregnancy stabbed me like a knife. I went back to pick up my daughter, not knowing what the future would hold—not knowing what to do.

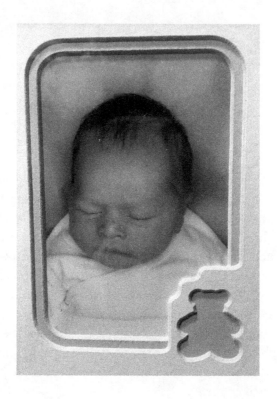

After some time, many discussions, and many more empty promises, we agreed to try again. Knowing what kind of person Chris could be and having faith that God was with us and had a plan for us, we continued to work on our marriage. The spring came and went, summer was here, and so was the baby's due date. We went into the hospital on June 30. The pregnancy was a relatively easy one, but the labor was not. I was expecting that we were going to go the C-section route again. But the doctors were persistent that we try to have a natural birth.

Our son, Zachary Adam, was born on July 1. As they cleaned him up and cleared his airways, I could sense that something was not to their liking. With the umbilical cord wrapped around his leg, the labor was long and didn't proceed as expected. The doctors were concerned because the baby was not breathing smoothly; he was grunting.

I lay on the hospital gurney, praying over and over again, "Just breathe. Please, Jesus, help him breathe." He was rushed to the NICU and monitored for a couple of days. It was a stressful time. I thanked God for the moment he was wheeled into my room in a traditional incubator and was allowed to stay with me for the remainder of our stay.

What a wonderful baby! Zachary was the total opposite of his sister. He was so easygoing, always smiling. What a change to put him down for a nap compared to his colic older sibling. As sad as it was to say, it was time for me to go back to work. My mother offered to leave her job and be the children's caregiver, while Chris and I were working. I was grateful that she was willing to do so.

Being a new mother again, leaving Soleil (now seventeen months) and Zachary (two months), was one of the hardest things to do. But having my mom there made it all possible. I don't think I would have been able to do it without her. Chris was still working all the crazy hours. Leaving my babies was not the only reason it was so difficult to return to work. Since I took extended maternity leave, I was informed that I was assigned to a new school and a new grade level, which added to the stress.

Trying to become acclimated to a new grade level, new school, and a new curriculum was quite a challenge because I was now placed in fourth grade, not second grade. The first week of school was difficult. My new classroom was in a portable trailer, which was not awful because my classroom had air conditioning; and I shared a bathroom with one other classroom, which was a real luxury. What made it difficult was that I was able to see all the families arrive each morning. There was one family who had a toddler that reminded me so much of Soleil. My eyes would well up seeing her golden curly locks, wishing I were home with my children.

However, at this time, finances were tight. Tight doesn't even come close to explaining how financially strapped we were, trying to dig ourselves back out of the hole of living on one paycheck and paying for health insurance because I didn't have insurance during my unpaid maternity leave.

Even though Chris's boss paid him his salary during his recovery from the dog attack, anyone in sales understands that you grow dependent on bonuses, and Chris wasn't getting those while he was out of work. Having a new baby and all the extra expenses involved with that made for an impossible budget to balance.

To my disappointment, I will confess that my mom was the financial obligation that frequently got overlooked or promised to be caught up on next week, next month. The sacrifice and hardship of not receiving what was promised put an additional strain on everyone. It took a long time to get back on our feet, never completely fulfilling our IOUs to my mom. So grateful for my parents' help, support, and sacrifice.

What?

Life continued. Both Soleil and Zachary ended up having surgeries. Soleil had eye surgery to help correct exotropia. Her eyes would drift outward when she looked at things in the distance or if she was tired. My parents watched Zachary for us. Chris and I brought Soleil to the hospital, sitting in the pre-op room in the children's hospital was torturous. Worries of what-ifs circled in my mind.

Trying to read to her and play with blocks to pass the time did not help. Chris decided to be the one to escort her into the operating room, a decision that I gratefully conceded to. We spent the time praying and holding hands while our daughter was in surgery. The doctor eventually came in and informed us that the surgery went well, and her eyes have remained straight ever since. Her 3D vision is nonexistent, but it doesn't impact her day-to-day vision; it only affects her enjoyment of 3D videos, which we feel is a fair trade off.

Zachary had a couple of surgeries as well. One scheduled, and one not. The planned surgery involved tendon transfers on all his toes. His tiny toes would curl under his foot. The orthopedic surgeon informed us that it was a condition that would cause him pain and discomfort for his entire life, and that he strongly advised the operation. His doctor was a gentle giant. This hunchbacked doctor had to have been over six feet tall, and he had the biggest hands I have ever seen.

As he explained the procedure he intended to do, I wondered how someone with such enormous fingers could work successfully on such little toes. It was a long, tedious surgery, waiting in that same surgical waiting room in the children's hospital that we occupied not so long ago for Soleil surgery. Gratefully, he came out with the comforting news that all went well. The recovery period was not an easy one. Zachary was left with two full-size casts from his toes up to his hips. Being only two, with the length of the recovery time, poor Zachary had to strengthen his muscles and learn to walk all over again, which he did through the grace of God and a little encouragement from his sister. He was determined to be able to retaliate and chase her after months of teasing and taunting, the only kind of motivation that a three-year-old sister can give.

The next surgery was the unexpected one. A few days before Halloween, Zachary was released from the hospital, discharged after a week of being treated, and cleared for pneumonia. We brought him to see my father-in-law dressed as a pumpkin matching his big sister. We rang the doorbell, and after a few pictures, it was apparent that Zachary was not feeling well. He was not himself—the usual happy little boy would not smile and just wanted to be held.

The next day, we called the pediatrician, and she ordered another x-ray. I was at work, so Chris ended up taking him. Unexpectedly, I was paged to the office; I had a call. It was my mom, and she was on her way to come to pick me up. "Zachary is going to the hospital. He's sick." My mom's voice was shaky, and she was crying. So I was picked up and met Chris at the hospital.

While at the imaging office, Chris received a call from the pediatrician, and she shared that the images were misread. She directed Chris to get the new imaging films immediately and take Zachary right to the hospital. "Don't wait for the ambulance. Just get him there now, Chris," were her directions.

Furious and worried, Chris tells me that he kicked the swinging door open, like a scene in an old-fashioned western movie, holding the fragile, limp Zachary in his arms on the search for the x-ray films. He shares later that as the doors swung open, Zachary whispered, "Get him, Dad," which I know must have empowered Chris to obtain the pictures and get Zachary to the hospital.

We found out later that not only were the x-rays misread, but that one of Zachary's lungs was filled with fluid. He needed to have a tube inserted to drain the fluid. While waiting for the procedure, they had to insert an IV. His little arms and his disappearing veins made it difficult, virtually impossible to get an IV started. Listening to his cries and watching the tears stream from his eyes tore me apart. Eventually, after prodding and poking both arms, the nurse was able to insert the line in a vein on the top of his tiny hand.

Waiting in the emergency room, doctors and nurses came in and took vitals and monitored him. One young doctor, probably envisioning himself as a Dr. McDreamy, came walking in and tried to hop over his IV line with his fancy clogs. The line got caught and yanked out. Witnessing the dangling IV line, his son's tiny bloody hand, and hearing Zachary's cries immediately sent Chris into a rage. His face reddened, and he yelled, "Get out of here!"

The doctor obnoxiously responded with, "Well, I'm the doctor." Chris sprang to his feet and was ready to take him out and give him a beating. It was chaos trying to calm Zachary and referee between Chris and the doctor as they had their confrontation. This was not the time or the place for such a scene; they looked like gesturing male peacocks marking their territory. The doctor finally agreed to leave, and we asked for another doctor.

After some time, the procedure was completed, a tube was inserted, and eventually, his lung was drained. Following a few days of observation and antibiotics, Zachary was allowed to go home. It was a critical introduction and lesson teaching us to be strong advocates for our family regarding medical treatment.

*****

Financially, with some adjustments, we were getting by. Then the next bomb dropped. Chris came home and informed me that he had lost his job. He also wanted to start a business with a coworker who also worked in construction, currently operating as a "one-man band." They thought that if they pooled their talents that it would be worth everyone's while.

We met with this man and his wife. They joined us for dinner. Sharing food and drink, sharing philosophies and stories, eased the worry of starting a business. That evening, they decided to start the construction company. As I feared, beginning the company did not help with the finances or the stability of our family.

Things went from bad to worse. We were encountering the coldest winter in years. The expansive house with the cathedral ceilings that we worked so hard to build was now impossible to heat. Our home was always cold, not healthy for the kids. My pay was the only consistent one. There was only one thing to do: sell the house. I felt defeated. How could we sell this house? We had put so much into this house, not just money, our time, our hearts, and souls.

Packing was devastating. This was my dream house. I loved everything that we built. From the circular drive to the Soft Play stoned play area with the redwood equipment to the potting shed that we renovated into a bunkhouse. Chris had nearly impaled himself working on that project when he fell off the ladder holding a bundle of shingles and falling between shards of glass that had broken off as we raised the roof of the shed. The glass fragments had landed, pointing up like one-foot crystal teepees. Was it all in vain?

So we put the house on the market, and our realtor ended up having a family that was interested in buying our home. Due to divorce, they were selling their house. They were looking for a place that would accommodate their family with an in-law and that had land for their horse. Our house fit the bill. We had initially built an apartment over the garage for my father-in-law or perhaps my parents when they got older. I never got to enjoy the garage because when we finished it and put on the garage door, the deal was sealed. After the paperwork was drafted and signed, it was time to leave.

It was the day of the final walkthrough. Chris left, leaving me by myself to conduct the inspection with the buyers and showing them through my home for one last time. The sadness that I felt as I led the walkthrough was difficult to hide. I walked them through the kids' room. Looking at the Winnie the Pooh mural that I had painted while I was pregnant with Soleil, I wondered if they were going to keep it or paint it over with a new coat of paint.

The new owner placed her hand on my shoulder, looked at me, and inquired if I was okay. She said she could tell that it was not an easy decision for me. I guess I have never been able to disguise my feelings very well. I just had hoped that Chris would be there with me. I felt abandoned.

After they left, I just sat on the window seat, looking out of the picture window and crying. Alone, crying inconsolably to the lyrics of the song "Landslide" by the Dixie Chicks. "Well, I've been afraid of changin'. Cause I built my life around you. Can I handle the seasons of my life?" Knowing the plans that I had, visions of hosting my daughter's wedding in the backyard, would never be was a devastating realization.

Gingerbread House

Where did we go next, you ask? Well, we passed this cute little house on our way every day as we dropped off the kids at daycare. It had a for-sale-by-owner sign posted in the front yard. We had considered buying it as an investment to renovate and flip it. So we made an appointment and made an offer on it before the closing of our home. It was a four-room house: no eat-in kitchen, no dining room, and only two small bedrooms. The house's square footage was the same size as our master bedroom suite in our last house.

Unfortunately, there was a brief time between the closings, which left us homeless. Having to have everything out of the house put us in a predicament. So Chris reached out to the owners of the new house. The owner gave Chris permission to move some things over in preparation of the renovations that would ensue following the closing.

In Chris's mind, it was just a matter of signatures and paperwork, so he directed that our belongings be moved into the four-car garage; however, I don't believe that the owner had the same understanding. I was unable to absorb any additional pressure, so I did not pay any attention to where things were going. Having to work full-time, pack everything, and take care of the kids, Chris reassured me that he would take care of everything else.

As we awaited the closing of our next house, Chris started prepping for the house's renovation. One morning, the owner stopped by. As he approached Chris, he noticed that the garage was packed. It was so filled that it appeared like it was bursting at the seams. The owner, distraught at the realization that the garage was filled, walked with Chris around to the backyard. Holding his head, he exclaimed, "What have you done? It looks like you already moved in!" Before he could even finish the word *in*, he caught a glimpse of the dog kennel that was holding Dakota. "You even brought the dog!" He was furious!

Eventually, after some negotiations, Chris and the owner came to the agreement that we would rent the property for a month. A price was decided upon and a check was written to ease the owner's worry. Within the month, we were able to purchase the little house, putting down a substantial down payment from the sweat equity proceeds from our last home. The new dwelling was so small Zachary named it the Gingerbread House. Starting renovations with two small kids, working full time as a teacher, and still trying to get the business off the ground presented us with problems.

Even after moving in, once the house was cleaned and painted, the garage was still packed with all our belongings because of the extreme downsizing. Chris decided to renovate the upstairs by flipping the basement stairs the opposite way to lead to the attic. It was tall enough for the children at the time, but the adults had to walk in the exact middle of the house to avoid hitting their head. It was not an easy venture, but we eventually put up paneling to hold up the insulation, painted everything white, and put down linoleum squares. It was a cute space. Chris even plumbed a bathroom space by reusing the original fixtures that we had removed from the existing downstairs bathroom for the kids. Perfect for them.

During this time, Chris was trying to balance the renovations of our home and the business' jobs. Unfortunately, during this time, drinking became a crutch. It was a way to fall asleep, a way to relax— just something to do. It got to the point that he and his crew would be drinking throughout the day.

During construction, we were living at my parents' house. You could cut the tension with a knife during our time there. To give everyone a break, we planned that we would camp out at the new house as a family. I packed dinner, got treats, and sleeping bags. I double-checked that we had everything we needed, grabbed some candles, and excitedly strapped the kids into their car seats in the minivan. The kids and I entered the house. But it was quiet. Way too quiet. I turned the corner to our soon-to-be bedroom and found Chris utterly passed out.

I yelled out, "What are you doing? What the hell! Nice!" He woke up in a stupor. He was still in his work clothes. I shuffled the kids back out of the house and put them back into the minivan with Chris following behind, trying to justify or explain. He stood in front of the minivan, pleading that we stay. "Just stay. It's all good!" I inched forward slowly because he wouldn't move away. Afraid to hit him but needing to go, I finally accelerated to a point to get out of there.

He lunged out of the way, and Soleil yelled, "You forgot Daddy!" I slowly drove back to my parents' house. What am I going to tell them? I dragged my feet, wishing I had money to take the kids to a hotel room and dreading what I will be faced with when I return with the kids. My fears were justified. "What are you doing back here?" "What a loser." "He's a deadbeat." There were no words of consolation from them. I had no justified retort. I humbly carried the kids upstairs and tucked them in. I found myself alone and cry-ing in my childhood room.

Eventually, the renovations were complete, and all was ready for us to move in. The queen-size bed that once was placed in a spare guest bedroom in the previous house now took up most of our bedroom space—no extra space in this room. To get around the bed, you had to shift sideways and shimmy along the bed. A metal farmer's stand was our makeshift shelving unit to hang our clothes because the closet was too narrow, and a regular-sized hanger would not fit in it. There was no room for anything else, no closet, no bureau, and no light. The room was so dark because it didn't have an overhead light. A desk light clamped to the metal farmers stand was the only light source as you entered the room.

Most of our clothes had to be stored down in the basement until we completed our addition plans. That presented a problem all of its own. There were no stairs to the basement because Chris had used them to get to the kids' space. To get down to the basement to do laundry, get supplies, or anything stored there, we had to walk outside, walk to the bulkhead, and then proceed to the basement. Our washing machine was not working, so I called a repairman to fix it. To my embarrassment, as I walked him to the cellar, he jokingly states, "Wow, all the comforts of home." I am sure that he didn't mean to hurt my feelings, but it hit me when I was down.

Princesses for the Princess

Little by little, we settled into our little house. Chris started a brief outpatient alcohol treatment. Insurance ends up not covering the program, so he stops going; but he tries hard to make things work. Things settled down, and we tried our best to continue to work on our relationship again. Soleil finished kindergarten at the school she was enrolled in before moving, and Zachary was in preschool. So for Zachary's birthday, we decided to go to Disney World.

To help defray the costs, my parents offered to come and help pay. The excursion was a welcomed distraction to the issues brewing. None of us wanted to face any of it. My mom went into travel agent mode and investigated all there is Disney. My parents booked the rooms and reserved a few dinners—one especially for Soleil: breakfast with the princesses. We decided to save money and drive. We all held it together during the eighteen-hour ride down. Each took turns driving, but Chris took the brunt of the responsibility.

We arrived and found our rooms. We had adjacent rooms so the kids could pass back and forth between them; having a TV in each room helped keep the peace. However, it was inevitable, and one afternoon, tempers flared over whether we should wait in line at the Buzz Lightyear exhibit or not. July's temperature and Chris's impatience justified skipping it. My parents' determination to get everything out of the trip and knowing how much Zachary loved *Toy Story* led to name-calling and a blowout. We ended up separating and going our separate ways for the rest of the day and the next. Guilt and a need to try to appease everyone was slowly eating at me.

Time does not heal all wounds, but at least they smooth things over. Things were calm enough so that we could civilly finish our week in Florida. We all enjoyed the princess breakfast; watching

Soleil marvel at the princesses made it all worth it. We also enjoyed a Hawaiian luau. The kids didn't seem to like the food but had the time of their lives playing the games. Races with spoons holding eggs and hula hooping were the distraction that we all needed.

The ride home was another story. We bought extra things, and we ran out of room in the minivan. Every inch, in and above the van was packed. We began the trek back to Massachusetts. Now with the excitement of the trip behind us, the ride home was not as fun. The van must have looked like the Flintstones' car, with the front of the minivan lifted due to all the excess weight in the back. Chris was determined to make the eighteen-hour ride into an eight-hour ride. I am not sure how we made it home. Racing home in such a manner, zig-zagging through traffic, my mother yelled in horror, "You are going to kill us. You are crazy."

Chris yelled back, "Just shut the f——k up." Poor Zachary started to feel sick. Not sure if it was the stress of the physical ride or the emotional worry, but I could tell he wasn't going to make it. It might have been mother's intuition, but I quickly reached for a plastic grocery bag. As I turned and opened the bag, Zachary projected his vomit right at me. Only through the grace of God did I somehow catch the vomit in the bag. It was like a scene from a cartoon. Little Zachary was in his car seat, strapped onto the back seat, and was projectile vomiting at me in the front seat holding up a bag. I still can't fathom how I was able to catch it all.

We pulled over, tied it up, and threw it out. Zachary felt better after that, Chris slowed down, and everyone was quiet. Once again, I believe that God's intervention gently reminded us to appreciate all that we have. I was grateful that my boy was feeling better and for the silence.

Investigation

Chris and his partner now had their own crew. It only consisted of a couple of men; however, it enabled them to work simultaneously on different jobs. Sort of divide and conquer. Chris picked up a junky old pickup truck so that he could travel from job to job. It would be better on gas, and that way, he could leave the work van filled with the tools at home or with the crew members on a job site.

At this point, we were again in the middle of another addition to our house. The mason had dug the basement hole. We had to lock and bolt the back door because the work site was immediately outside of it. We were not worried about Soleil because she could not maneuver the old latch, but Zachary could work his magic. He could skillfully open and unlock it like a bank robber breaking into a safe. He worried me because he would stand at the door and watch the workers.

One afternoon, after school, I heard him yell, "Kota! No!" I ran to him, and to my horror, I realized that he just witnessed Dakota try to jump over the hole. Dakota was now eight years old and was having skin problems. The vet had explained that the medication prescribed made the dog feel like he could do anything. He felt like super dog, but he wasn't!

Poor Zachary witnessed Dakota fall into the hole. Our pet lay there motionless. The mason called Chris, and he came home in his little pickup truck. It was a sad evening; my heart dropped watching Chris holding Dakota as they were lifted out of the hole in the excavator's bucket. With help, Chris placed our beloved pet in the pickup and raced to the vet.

Hours later, he returned red-eyed and distraught. They couldn't save him. Being bombarded by the question "Where's Kota?" and the sad, pleading eyes searching for answers made it difficult for Chris to handle. It wasn't easy trying to comfort the children. This was their first experience of loss. Dakota was always there, protecting and watching them ever since they were born.

We lost track of time that day. Eventually, it hit us: "Where's the crew? Why haven't they brought the van home?" Chris started making calls to his partner, calling the workers and their families— no sign of them. Chris went to the work site: no van. Chris called the police and told them the situation. Days go by, and no sign of the two workers or the van.

It's the day before Thanksgiving, and Chris was asked to go to the police station. I had the day off from work, so I went with him. They sat us down, and before they started asking Chris questions, he was read his rights. It became apparent that Chris was being interrogated for the disappearance of the workers and the van. I sat there dumbfounded, thinking that maybe we were on some comedy show, like the ones that prank unsuspecting people. But this was not funny! It was scary, and it was happening.

Questions repeatedly posed to him by the detectives. "How were the employees able to move the van? Where are they?" I couldn't believe my ears. During the interrogation, the detective asked if they could inspect the foundation hole and the yard. My head was spinning at this point. Did they think that we buried the van and bodies somewhere on our property? Do they think we would bury them in our foundation, under our house, and where our children live? What?

The police continued their investigation, even questioning the mason and those who dug the hole for the addition. These were people that we have known and did business with since the first little cottage. Chris knew these people for years; how embarrassing to receive calls from them telling us that they were questioned by the police about the employees' disappearances. How could this happen? Things could not get any worse.

It was the holiday season; I'm the only one working—no tools, no jobs for Chris, and even his partner was not supporting him. Since the van was gone, he needed to make sure that the pickup truck was running reliably. Christmas Eve, Chris returned home from the local tire store. He returned home not able to walk or stand up straight. "I just had a couple of drinks while I waited for the tires to be completed," he informed me. No money, it's the holidays, the kids are still grieving over the loss of Dakota, the police are still investigating Chris, my parents' frustration over our troubles was escalating, he is drinking, and I don't know what to do.

*****

Since Chris was looking for jobs and interviewing, we thought it was best if I used the pickup truck and he took the minivan. It was a two-wheel-drive pickup covered with more rust than paint and the loudest exhaust I have ever heard. No money available to fix it, I had to swallow my pride and make do. It would get me to work, and that was what the priority was at the moment.

I remember trying to get home after work one day, waiting in the school's car dismissal line with parents and students walking past me. I sat there as the truck sputtered and backfired; unable to hide or sink any lower in the seat, I just sat there. I plastered on a smile and waved to the families as they look to see who in the world would be driving such a piece of junk. It was the hardest thing to do. How embarrassing to be the one sitting in this monstrosity, wishing to be invisible, and wishing to be able to escape.

Making things worse was when I would reminisce back to when Chris was doing well, working at the dealership as a sales manager. During those years, I was able to drive the pick of the lot. Many years driving brand-new top-of-the-line SUVs, now spending many nights of woe asking, "What have I done to deserve this?" Often I would try to disguise my disappointments by joking that I must have done something wrong in my past life to deserve this. Of course, it's not something I truly believed, but I have heard of various religions threatening reincarnation punishments for poor life choices. It was a way to make light of my circumstances and help me deal with and accept humbling times.

With the financial problems mounting, Chris got a job as an auction promotor. With his connections in the car business, his assignment was to sign up dealerships to become part of and use this auction. The location was in Boston, so he had to travel to work, driving all around Massachusetts to solicit the dealerships. So he continued using the minivan at this time because it presented better than the junky pickup truck. To deal with the pressures, Chris resorted to his comfort crutch: alcohol. I found blackberry brandy bottles hidden under the minivan seats. When asked why I smell it on his breath, he dismissed it and made up lies, telling me that it was cough medicine.

Each time I tried to bring up the question, he made up another lie. I received a call one evening, and it was Chris; he was in an accident and needed to be picked up. When the details of the accident are revealed, I learn that he was under the influence. What more do I have to take?

After a talk—well, not a civil discussion but a screaming match—I demand that he leaves. He is not allowed to return until he gets help—real help—and stops drinking. He packed his duffel bag, and I'm brokenhearted as I watch him walk down the street with his belongings slung over his back. But I needed to do what I had to do to protect my children. It was not fair for them to be brought up in a family fighting and arguing all the time. I also did not want them to see their father struggling with his "alcohol demons" as they got older. It was not in their best interest to watch that and grow up thinking that that type of behavior was acceptable.

Ultimatum

Chris signed up for a weeklong alcohol treatment program in Providence. In his absence, his license was suspended, meaning he couldn't drive. So he ended up staying at his sister's house; he was lucky to have her assistance getting back and forth to daily sessions. During this time, I tried to keep our daily schedules as consistent as possible with support from my parents. The kids missed their father but seemed reassured that he was to return from the hospital very soon.

During this time, Chris's sister vehemently advocated for her brother and voiced her opinions with me. She was under the belief that I had no right kicking Chris out of his house. It was his house, and he had as much right to stay in it as I did. She finally ended our conversation with, "You can't shield them (meaning my kids) from everything."

Well, maybe I couldn't shelter them from everything, but I certainly would do my best. It was not an easy decision to make, but I had to choose my children over my husband. Our fighting and his drinking were not the makings of a healthy atmosphere for them to live in. It was disappointing that I did not have her support; it was so challenging to stick by the decision demanding that he receive treatment for my children's sake.

At this point, I felt so alone. My parents continued to be supportive and were there for the children but were now sick and tired of the drama that came with Chris and his issues. Very willingly, my parents shared their dismay and disappointment with my choices. Being embarrassed with my situation, I did not seek comfort from my friends. I continued to work, trying my best to disguise and hide my troubles, ending each night with questioning prayers of why.

However, it was my responsibility to provide stability and consistency that my children needed. I needed to protect my children from the problems and heartache that I was dealing with. They deserved the chance to be kids and not be privy to adult problems. After one of the counseling sessions, I had met with Chris, allowing him to see the children. I brought Chris back to his sister's house and returned to our home.

Forty minutes later, when I got home, the kids were asleep in their car seats. I had to unbuckle them and carry each of them into the house, which was not an easy feat—at this point, being five and six years old. My chubby kids were heavy. Huffing and puffing, frequent breaks were necessary, resting my sleeping babies on my knee and praying to make it up the steep stairs to the loft. Cursing as I banged my head on the low pitch of the ceiling, I placed them in their beds. Once they were safe and sound tucked in their bed, I got right to preparing things for the next day. I busily got to work making lunches, setting out clothes, correcting papers, and looking over my plans for the next day of teaching.

After the busy day and night, I was ready to sit down and regroup; but as they say, no rest for the weary, because all of a sudden, the phone rang. I answered the phone, a call from Chris saying that he and his sister argued. She was communicating to him that he had every right to stay in his house. "How dare she ask you to leave your house? She has no right to keep you out of your house." She continued to preach her view.

At this point, Chris—perhaps with all the help during his program—realized that his actions were not conducive to a healthy, happy environment for his children. Angered that her brother was supporting me ignited the situation. To add fuel to the fire, her husband was trying to get a new job. Her husband was worried that the investigation regarding the van and the workers was still open.

Concerned that having Chris at the house or having any connection to an open case would harm his chances of getting the job clinched the decision. Chris was no longer welcome to stay, and he had to leave. He informed me that he was packed up and was heading out, and once he found a place, he would let me know where he was. "Perhaps I'm meant to walk the earth," he says to me.

It was January, and the temperature was dropping. I couldn't leave him out in the elements. That night, I had to wake up each of the kids again, dress them up, pack them back into the rental car that I was driving due to the minivan's accident, and go looking for him. I eventually found him. There he was, sitting on that duffel bag in the dark. Shivering, bundled up in a winter coat, he jumped into the passenger seat gratefully, leaving his resting place by the highway's off-ramp.

I agreed to let him stay at home while he finished the program. He would have to ride the bus to get to the hospital because I had to get the kids ready for school and go to work. He decided to ride a bike to the hospital because there weren't any buses that went directly to where he needed to go. It was faster and more direct to ride his bike.

One night, he came home with a story that I will never forget. Since it was winter, during icy mornings, the New England streets were sanded for driving safety. On his way home, he reached an elevation and started coasting down. However, to his dismay, his bike was speeding down the hill. As the cycle picked up speed, the tires were slipping on the sand, which interfered with the ride. He was going so fast at that moment that he was not able to steer the bike, and the tire nudged the curb. That nudge sent him totally out of control. He continued to verbally paint the picture of him trying to gain control.

In my mind's eye, I could see his legs waving in the air; his feet on and off of the pedals; and hands on and off the handlebar, trying to get balance and not crash. Somehow he made it safely down the hill without any harm except to his ego. As he told his story, I found myself giggling and shaking my head. I could visualize his ordeal. He did not appreciate me laughing, but it was nice to have a light-hearted moment. I once again realized how blessed he was. Protected by God, I felt bad for his poor guardian angel.

Chris completed the program. We participated in some couple counseling as well. Chris was diagnosed with a mood disorder during his discharge from the program. Medication was prescribed, and continued treatment was recommended. We were working it out, he was attending AA meetings, and the kids were thrilled to have their dad back.

Do It Again, Daddy

After a brief stint at selling cars, Chris turned his attention back to the addition. The project had been put on hold for quite a while. The stalled addition consisted of the foundation that was the site that caused the demise of our beloved Dakota back in the fall. Finally, after the police searched the property, we were allowed to backfill the hole around the foundation and had put down planks for a floor. It provided us with a great backyard porch. Not much to look at, but it made do.

The porch connected the back of the existing house to the detached garage. We decided to add a front entrance connecting both of the structures. The neighbors must have had such a show. Each day, we worked to build the floor and put up the roof with only the two of us and a nail gun. The beams and headers teetering and wobbling above us certainly were being held by our guardian angels. Using our body weight to counterweight and balance the construction was similar to a child's metal teetering toy sold in museum gift shops.

The kids growing up in a constant state of construction seemed right at home. One day while we were working, the kids kept themselves busy. They had found a way to readjust some two-by-tens, wooden planks to make a seesaw. That kept them busy for quite a while. Then Soleil discovered that the seesaw could be used as a catapult. Zachary and Soleil took turns placing their stuffed animals on one end and then jumping on the other end. To their delight, the stuffed animal would be sent sailing through the air.

Periodically, I would look over to check on them. I noticed it was Zachary's turn to place the stuffed animal on the catapult; as he stepped back, the toy shifted and fell off. He quickly went back to

58

prop it up, and to my horror, I saw Soleil running and becoming airborne. Not being able to stop, she hit the catapult, sent the two by ten right into Zachary's chin, and hit the bottom of his nose. He started screaming with blood running down his face.

In such pain, he started sprinting around the house. Chris and I started chasing him as he wailed in pain, hands flailing, running circles around the house. Eventually, we were able to catch him. Covered in blood, wincing in pain, and hyperventilating, we tried to soothe him. Compresses and nasal packs eventually stopped the bleeding, and he was calm. Once again, narrowly escaping a perilous situation. The force of the trauma could have been fatal if it hit at another angle.

*****

Following that incident and with the physical needs exceeding my capabilities, we acknowledged that we needed more assistance. We were able to hire a local handyman who was out of work and willing to be paid by the day. It was a double-edged sword because the more he worked helping Chris meant less money getting us further away from completing the addition. We decided that a roof and walls would be an acceptable target for completion with the money we had.

It was a lovely summer day. I watched Soleil and Zachary as they swam in the little blue Intex blow-up pool. Chris and the handyman had put up the roof headers and roof rafters. Their goal for the day was to attach the plywood to the roof.

As Chris carried a sheet of plywood across the roof, his foot got tangled by the nail gun's air hose. Chris yells out, "S——t!" and we all looked in his direction. It was like slow motion. He tripped and fell onto the sheet of plywood. Spread across the plywood, he slid down the roof and glided smoothly through the air like he was Aladdin on a magic carpet. We all sat in astonishment as he held onto the plywood and sailed many feet away from the house.

Once the plywood lost its air support, Chris and the sheet of wood came crashing down. I walked over and nonchalantly asked whether he was okay or if he needed me to call the ambulance. We joke to this day how the kids were amused, clapping and yelling, "Do it again, Daddy!" The handyman was amazed to see how calmly and in a matter-of-fact manner that I checked on Chris. I guess by this point, after years into our journey, experiences had hardened me not to be reactionary and that I now found that I was gaining the ability to address stress or emergencies calmly.

Summer came and went. I returned to work, and Chris continued to work on the house. I came home to news that I was not expecting. Chris shared that while he was organizing the garage, a vehicle pulled into the driveway abruptly. Chris approached the driver and noticed that it was the police detective that was in charge of the investigation. He informed Chris that the van and the workers were located. One of the workers turned himself in earlier, and the final worker was found and arrested down south. When the van was found, it was empty. The tools were later found at local pawnshops. They were sold by the thieves to provide them with money for their getaway. The detective offered his apologies for any inconveniences caused by the investigation and stated that the case was now closed.

Later, when the worker's trial approached, we were asked how we wanted to proceed and asked to write a victim statement. We were informed that the victim statement was to be considered in sentencing following the trial. Knowing that he had young children, we wrote a letter stating that we would support a sentence sending him to a drug treatment center. Once he was back on his feet, we were led to believe that he would make payments of restitution.

While on bail, this individual ran and disappeared again. So we never received any compensation for the tools or the money lost from the theft. Unfortunately, to this day, we are not sure what happened to him. His actions caused damage to our reputations, created hurt and challenging times in our relationship, and brought stress to our family financially and emotionally. Fortunately, that was another season in our lives that was done and over with. Case closed!

Happy Birthday!

Slowly but surely, our savings dwindled. In attempts to complete the addition, we sold a parcel of land that Chris had purchased before we were married, and we cashed in all my savings bonds. It was not easy, but we were getting by. I was working full-time, and Chris was now exclusively working on the house. It was reassuring to have Chris home, sober and attentive. It was nice to have him home to help with family responsibilities, present at family meals, and I appreciated the brief reprieve of being responsible for the day-to-day familial duties.

Enjoying our daily interactions as a family helped to recharge us to face our next curveball. It was my birthday; my parents joined us for brunch at one of my favorite restaurants. It was a lovely celebration. However, I didn't feel well after. Jokingly, as my mom walks me into the house, she asks, "You aren't pregnant, are you?"

To our surprise, a home pregnancy test confirmed that I was truly going to be a mom again. I was happy but worried at this point—so many concerns. We were just about getting by; how could we support another mouth to feed? I was thirty-five, which was considered an advanced age for pregnancy. Even though we had hoped for another baby, we had given up on that possibility—all the baby items donated or given away. We didn't even have a crib!

Four months later, we decided to share the news with the kids with the first trimester behind us. Soleil was so excited to be a big sister. Now in third grade, what could be better than having a baby in the family? She was convinced that we were going to have a girl. During my other two pregnancies, we never found out what sex the baby was. Since I was older now, prenatal genetic testing was recommended. Since this was our last child, we decided to find out the sex of the baby during one of the appointments. The doctor scheduled the appointment, and since this impacted the whole family, we brought Soleil and Zachary with us.

To Soleil's disappointment, the technician informed us that we were having a baby boy. With tears streaming down her face, Soleil broke down and cried. "Are you sure? It has to be a girl. I want a sister!"

Zachary, on the other hand, was ecstatic! "Yes! A brother!" With our newest addition on the way, our family excitedly worked together to prepare the nursery and babyproof the house. As the due date approached, we needed to decide on a name. As a teacher, naming a child can be tricky—so many names bring back memories that a teacher would rather forget. Many nights were spent looking through the baby books. Reading the names and their meanings were nightly events. Everyone with their favorites, advocating and trying to get the other family members on board.

Tucker was Chris's choice. Determined to wear me down, it was always at the top of his list. That was one fight I was not going to lose. I was vehemently against the name Tucker. Many unflattering rhyming words were associated with it. All I could envision were difficult elementary and middle school years for our child being teased and taunted by bullies. A red line consistently crossed that name off the list.

One name that we did agree on was Morgan. Being fans of the movie Wyatt Earp, we loved the name of the main character's brother, Morgan, but we were unsure whether we liked the alliteration of using the letter M for both the first and last name. We decided on a name but kept it close to our hearts to share only once he was born.

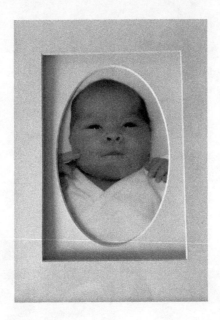

Our time waiting for our little one flew by, hoping that the baby would come early since it was my third pregnancy. No luck; he was very comfortable where he was, making me quite uncomfortable. While we waited, we were blessed by family and friends who lovingly and generously helped us prepare for our little boy. My mom threw a baby shower at our favorite buffet restaurant. Soleil was in her glory, the perfect big sister helping with all the preparation.

Along with that event, my teammates at work surprised us with another baby shower at school. With the crib and the changing table located at a consignment shop, we were ready! Finally, November 10 arrived, bringing our beautiful baby boy. He was brought into this world by cesarean section delivery. We welcomed him into our family and named him Samuel Morgan. Samuel, which means "God heard" in Hebrew. Which is exactly what Sam is: an answer to our prayers.

Happy Holidays

At this point, Chris was a stay-at-home dad. He was caring for Baby Sam and conducting himself better than Mr. Mom himself. He ended up having some pain and redness in his leg. It was the leg that sustained the damage from the dog attack back so many years ago. He was evaluated and diagnosed with phlebitis. He would have to spend a few days in the hospital to receive antibiotic infusions.

On December 23, it was evident that he was not going to be home for Christmas. I was determined to keep things consistent, so I brought the kids to see Chris and then we went to Our Lady of La Salette Shrine to attend mass and light a candle for Chris's recovery. When we got home, the kids went into the house to prepare for bedtime. I remained outside to shovel and attempt to chip some ice apart in the driveway with a type of ice pick in anticipation of family visiting Christmas Eve. My neighbor, who was snow-blowing his driveway, started to walk his blower across the road and toward our house. To my dismay, I watched him walk toward me. He waved and walked right past me to go to another neighbor's driveway, who had his own plow truck. I'm not sure if my eyes welled up because of the cold or because he didn't offer any help. Being too proud, I didn't appeal for help, and I continued to shovel and attempt to clear the driveway with my primitive shovel and ice pick.

Suddenly, Soleil frantically calls me; I run in to find her pointing at the TV room. Since the gutters were frozen, the snow that was melting on the roof had built up and had nowhere to go. The ceiling was stained with waterlines, marks indicating that the plaster and the ceiling board had been absorbing the leakage during the day.

Now totally saturated, the ceiling was releasing the water as clouds do; it was raining in our house. Water dripped through the recessed lighting and all over the new large screen TV that my parents just charged on their credit card for us, and we hadn't even started to pay off yet. Berserk that the water would blow the lights or affect the electricity. "What do I do? Should I turn off the lights?"

Panic-stuck and unsure as to what I should do, I call Chris, and he tells me that he will call for a taxi to bring him home. After some negotiations, he calls his friend Wes, and I call a family friend for help. Thank God my friend sends her husband, and Wes shows up. They shovel off the flat roof, and the indoor rain shower stops. The men leave, and I finally put the kids to bed.

I called Chris to reassure him that everything was okay. So thankful for our friends' assistance. So grateful for the kindness of others. I'm not sure what I would have done. I got a bucket of floor cleaner and a rag and started to wash the floor so that it could dry while the family was sleeping. I find myself sighing and wondering to myself, "How could things get any worse?"

As I mutter the words silently, the lights abruptly go out. I am suddenly surrounded by darkness. The electricity went out! I started crying, trying to finish what I had started. Feeling completely defeated, asking, "What more do I have to endure? Why is all this happening to me?" I dragged myself to my bedroom and went to sleep weeping.

Strength

Chris's leg symptoms returned and were worse. He was only home for a short period before he was readmitted to the hospital once again. This time, it was much more severe. His leg had a staph infection, phlebitis, and cellulitis. Reassured that, after a series of antibiotics, he would be discharged helped me to carry on. Fatigued and hopeful, I returned home from work anticipating a call or some word that Chris was ready to be picked up from the hospital.

When I got into the house, I found my mom rocking Sam. He was two years old at this point. This was unexpected because they were home early. Sam was in early intervention because he was a late talker, and he was supposed to attend a playgroup. My mom explained that they left the playgroup early because Sam wouldn't stand up. "He just kept raising his hands and wanted to be held. He didn't seem like he was feeling well, Rita!" I didn't pay much attention to it, attributing his behavior to missing his dad. Chris was his primary caregiver at this point. However, his symptoms escalated. Something was wrong. My parents agreed to stay with Soleil and Zachary, and I ended up taking him to the children's emergency room.

It was hours and hours of waiting in the emergency room. Sitting on the hard plastic chairs, holding and rocking a crying baby, was physically and emotionally draining. I felt like crying myself at a certain point. I looked across the emergency room, and I saw someone very familiar. Were my eyes playing tricks on me? No, it was Chris.

Chris was walking through the ER in his johnny with an IV hanging and walking toward us. I was so relieved and angry at the same time. I wanted to start crying even more at this point and wanted him to be there with me. But then reality hits: What is he doing? He needs to be in his room getting treatment for his leg.

After some time of holding Sam, he agrees to return to his hospital room. He kisses Sam and me on the forehead and leaves. Every ounce of my being wants to yell, "No, don't go!" but I have to be strong! He leaves, and eventually, we are brought into the triage room in the ER. At first, the doctors believed that Sam was constipated. However, after a night of standing up, rocking him in my arms, and an x-ray, to my horror, I am informed that he has cysts on his intestines. The cysts were twisted and blocking his intestines, requiring immediate emergency surgery.

Each of my children have had some health scares as youngsters. Soleil had eye surgery. Zachary had tendon surgery on all his ten toes and then was hospitalized because of pneumonia complications requiring a tube inserted into his lung to drain fluid. So we were not strangers to surgeries, but there was time to process the stress, and Chris was always there, and now, I was alone.

Sam and I were escorted to a waiting room in the hospital as dawn approached. The surgery had to be scheduled, and the surgeon needed to be prepped. By this time, my mom joined us. She accompanied me as Sam was wheeled into the surgical prep room. My baby was lying there looking so weak and helpless. God bless her soul, being one of the most sensitive, emotional women I know; my mom didn't want me to be alone. However, my worries were compounded seeing my mom sobbing and crying while rubbing Sam's little arm, providing me the strength to overcome my worries once again. I needed to be strong for my son and now my mom as well.

We all waited patiently; it seemed like an eternity. Eventually, the doctor came up and informed us that Sam was okay, that the bowel resection was complete, and that they took out his appendix as well because it was infected. Sam remained in the hospital for a few days, and I stayed with him.

Meanwhile, Chris was discharged and was able to join us in the hospital. He visited during the day and returned home at night to take care of Zachary and Soleil. Sam's recovery went well, and he was allowed to return home. As I placed Sam onto his bed, a feeling of gratitude and relief overcame me, so thankful to be home with my entire family.

Bank

During the time Chris was in the hospital receiving treatments for his leg, I called our mortgage company, realizing that our payment, if not due, would soon be due. I inform them of our problems and assure them that we would get everything back on track once Chris was home. He is the "money man" of the family and takes care of the bills.

Hearing the issues, they offer help in the form of a modification. They informed me that we might qualify for assistance. When Chris returned home, he called the mortgage company and requested that they send us paperwork to review. After reading the guidelines, we completed the paperwork and submitted them. The bank sent a notice stating that we qualified for the modification program. The letter said that all we needed to do was to complete three trial modification payments, and once those payments were made, if made on time, we would be given a new adjusted mortgage payment. Little did we know how this offer would greatly impact us later on and have such a devastating outcome on our family.

Each month, mortgage payments were made using the bank's speed pay system, which were automated withdrawals. These authorized withdrawals from our bank account were made directly to the bank. The requirements of the proposed modification of making the three payments were fulfilled, and we continued to make monthly payments. The bank finally notified us that we completed the trial and would be receiving paperwork. Expecting the final paperwork for the modification, we were blindsided by the events that followed. We received the paperwork, but it wasn't what we expected. It was not the modification paperwork; it was a notification that the program was no longer offered. We were then put into two other modification programs that were either discontinued or no longer available. During this time, we trustingly and naively continued to authorize the "speed pay" monthly mortgage payments.

In November 2009, Chris called to make the mortgage payment over the phone as he usually did. But this time, the payment was not accepted. Transferred to a representative, Chris was informed that they, the bank, would not accept payments and that the mortgage company was filing for foreclosure. The payments that were withdrawn from our bank account were never applied to our mortgage. The bank denied receipt of the money even though our bank statements proved that money was withdrawn from our account and taken by the bank. For months following, Chris would call daily, trying to rectify the mistake. He was unable to speak to the same person; no one to send the paperwork to, no one to direct copies of our bank statements to. He retold our story every day to new people who offered no help. Their suggestions were to keep submitting the paperwork. We sent the packets over and over again, feeling like we were in an evil version of the movie *Groundhog Day*.

Doing the same thing over and over again, jumping through every hoop that we were directed to jump through with nothing to show. Even attempting to have the documents signed for, we would send FedEx packets repeatedly. Adding to our frustration, the return receipts came back signed with joke names like Sandy Bottoms or illegible signatures. Since Chris was home and I was at work, he worked on it each day, never speaking to the same person and never getting the same response or guidance. The stress was having its effect on Chris.

Soleil was in middle school at this point. One day, she entered the house to find Chris sitting at the table, unable to speak or lift his head. Soleil called 911. He was brought to the hospital, and the doctors determined that he had suffered a TIA mini-stroke. The following months tested us all; daily calls of foreclosure and threats of evictions followed by additional calls on the same day from different departments of the mortgage company, directing us to complete more paperwork and send more documents promising resolution of our problems. All were conflicting with each other.

Read All about It!

Stressful is not even close to describing our lives at this point, not knowing what would happen each day with no ability to control or fix the problem. Moreover, during our fight with the bank, we were forced to acknowledge Zachary's school struggles. Eventually, we decided to have him evaluated. The evaluation resulted in a diagnosis of dyslexia and ADHD.

We were fortunate to find free tutoring. Their teachers were trained in a specialized program to address dyslexic student learning needs. Elementary school consisted of multiple yearly TEAM meetings. Middle school started, and Zachary began to verbalize feelings of inferiority and depression. The day he said that he would rather die than go to school was when we acknowledged the severity of the problem.

After some time, we determined that he would benefit from a specialized school to address his learning challenges. Facing the problems that my son was struggling with devastated me. Torturous reflections tore at me. "How is it that my son doesn't have the tools to be an effective learner? How is it that I can't support him to feel confident to go to school? What can I do to help him not identify himself as a stupid person? What kind of teacher am I?" I felt like a failure, many sleepless nights. I would wake up in the middle of the night to do more research, making every effort to find a solution to help my son.

Chris was prescribed medications to address his mood condition that the medical experts diagnosed years before during the alcohol treatment program. The medication's side effects created additional problems; he was falling asleep during the day and was awake at night. Our family grew accustomed to Chris's problems staying awake during the day.

During IEP meetings and dinners, he would doze off. I would try to pinch or nudge him, but it was fruitless. It was worrisome during the times that he would struggle to stay awake while driving. The kids took turns keeping a watchful eye on him. Similar to flamingos, it was amazing to watch how Chris perfected the ability to sleep standing up.

One morning, he woke me up, holding a washcloth to his forehead. His face was covered with blood. He informed me that he was heading to the hospital to get stitches. Not sure if it was exhaustion or frustration, but I didn't even offer to drive him. Insensitively, I sent him on his way with a goodbye and "You better be back before the kids have to go to school because I can't take time out." Fortunately, he was! At first, they wanted to keep him for observation because he had shared his inability to stay awake. Quickly, Chris changed his report to tripping on a toy. Unable to keep him there, his injury was stitched up, and he was sent home.

With the additional financial demands and pressures of the extra educational expenses, Chris decided to get a paper route job. It was not a glorious position, but Chris was willing to do it. Since he couldn't sleep at night, he could deliver papers early in the morning, get the kids off to school, and then sleep during the day. At first, it seemed like a great idea. He would quietly leave for work in the early a.m. He would complete his route and return before the kids had to go to school. But during this short-lived job, Chris once again put his guardian angel to work.

One winter morning, Chris was heading to the newspaper distribution center. It was snowing again; our location had been hit by several storms one after another. The roads were narrow and lined with walls of plowed snow, now frozen walls of ice.

As Chris entered onto a highway, he was suddenly broadsided by a plow. The plow clipped the car's bumper in such a way that Chris was dragged for a time. However, to Chris's horror, the lane he was in no longer existed. It was more of an ice ramp. The giant plow slingshot him up and over the ice ramp. The car shot in the air, just like Evil Knievel. The snow covered the windshield, making it impossible to see what was going on.

When the car hit the ground, Chris turned on the windshield wipers, forcing him to realize that...yikes! He was in the middle of the highway on the other side, facing the wrong direction. Somehow he was able to get the car to the side of the highway without being hit. I got a call from Chris later. He was safe, but the car was being towed, and he explained his experience. The tow truck driver was kind enough to bring Chris to his garage location.

During this drive, Chris had the opportunity to hear the driver's story, which he shared with us later that evening. This kind man who has helped him had custody of his six-year-old. During his night shifts, the son accompanied his dad, did homework on the bench seat, and slept in the truck at night because there wasn't anyone to take care of him. This story helped us to be grateful that we still have each other, which helped to reduce the blow of the car's loss.

Chris tries again, and he continues to deliver papers. The doctors continue to monitor and tweak his medications. Giving him a pill to help him sleep and another one to wake him up. I was preparing to go to work—no show from Chris. Suddenly the phone rings, and it's a police officer. He informs me that Chris was in an accident. He tells me that Chris hit a telephone pole and was being transported to the local hospital for evaluation. Back in emergency mode, I frantically make breakfast, get the kids ready, and call into work that I would be late.

During this time, Chris was able to call from the hospital and reassure me that he was okay, he was going to be released, and that he would get a ride home. I brought the children to school, breathed a sigh of relief, and went to work. Later that evening after work, sitting with Chris I learned the specifics of the crash. His guarding angel once again protected him. If he had hit at a slightly different angle, the accident's outcome would have been very different. Thank you, God, for that intervention! More bills heading our way: ambulance drive, hospital care, and a bill from the utility company for telephone pole repair, but Chris was alive and home.

Vacations

During the years since Samuel was born, the family had not been able to take official vacations. My parents were often gracious enough to assist us with booking a suite at a hotel that we enjoyed visiting in Old Orchard Beach in Maine. It usually was booked during Memorial Day so that the entire family, including my parents, could combine celebrating our anniversary, my father's birthday, and have a little getaway. The kids enjoyed the heated pool and the amusement rides. We all savored the fruits of the sea. Not the most ideal way to celebrate an anniversary, but it was worth it as we watched the kids enjoy themselves. You could see the happiness beam from Soleil as she had beads braided into her hair. Having bragging rights when she returned to school was the ultimate.

However, as the kids got older, contention grew that we never went anywhere. Once again, we were able to count our blessings. Chris's older sister still lived in East Hampton. "Bring the kids and stay with us. Come enjoy the Hamptons!" The offer from his sister was music to our ears. For years we accepted the offer of a weeklong beach vacation. We would try to book the last week in August before school started. It was a glorious way to end the summer, recharge before school, and of course, get a lovely tan. The latter was my gauge as to how the vacation went. The darker the tan meant the nicer weather, allowing more time at the beach and by the pool.

As the kids got older, the trip to see Auntie and Uncle was a treasured tradition. Shopping for all the treats to bring for the week was part of the fun. We couldn't afford to buy it there or eat at restaurants there either. It was too expensive! Bins and coolers of food were purchased and bought for a week of indulgences. The ferry ride across the Long Island Sound was always eventful and like a trip of its own.

The time spent in Long Island, creating memories and taking pictures of all the summer fun, were gifts from God. The beach provided a perfect backdrop for photo opportunities while fishing, walking on the beach, and making sand castles. We would marvel to watch Soleil dodge the crashing waves of the sea. Many days were spent enjoying the sun at an inlet watching the sailboats as they set off on a voyage through the canal, wondering where they were going and dreaming of what it would be like to be along for the sail. The boys had such fun searching for special seashells and chasing fiddler crabs across the sand in a protected cove. Chris's sister had kayaks for all to use; we had so much fun floating and playing peekaboo through the tall seagrass as the tides changed. There was no better way to enjoy summer days.

The kids anxiously anticipated the trips into town to visit the candy shop, where every type of candy possible was available. Their eyes became as wide as saucers as they scanned the old-fashioned penny candy jars. Shelves of containers filled with chocolates, gummies, and jawbreakers. Eating their favorite chicken dinner at the annual firemen's BBQ was the highlight gathering of the trip. No matter how I tried, not ever being able to make chicken and roasted potatoes taste as good as it did from there. Toasting marshmallows for s'mores by the fire and playing card games, and listening to music was the perfect ending to glorious days. Thankful because, financially, we could not afford a family trip or vacation, but also eternally grateful for the time and the chance to create such happy memories each summer with my children and Chris's family.

Can You See That?

T ime went on, and we had a sort of reprieve. Little did we know we were in the eye of another storm. Chris needed some new glasses. He went to the local ophthalmologist for a checkup and a new eyeglass prescription. There was something unusual about the results, so Chris was referred to a doctor at the Rhode Island Eye Center.

Since he would be having his eye dilated, I took the day out of work to drive him and attend the appointment with him. After the appointment, we could get a bite to eat since it was in the heart of Providence. Little did we know what was in store for our family. The tests identified a tumor. One that would need to be monitored. As time went on, with each appointment, the tumor grew. The location and growth of it were critical, and the doctor referred Chris to a specialist in Boston.

The tumor grew to the point that required surgery. The doctor explained that they were not sure if the tumor was benign or malignant. However, testing it to evaluate it might cause blindness. It only made sense to eliminate the tumor. Loss of vision would result, but at least the growth would be removed. Chris had to face the realization that he was going to lose the vision in one eye. The procedure and the results of the gamma knife were explained but not the details. Perhaps for good reason.

Chris and his sister headed out early the morning of the surgery. I remained home to care for the kids. Updates were sent via text messages and pictures. We spent the day praying that all would go smoothly, that the surgery would be successful. We received a text that all was good and that they were heading home. Eventually, Chris returned home with his head and eye wrapped with gauze and bandages. That night, Chris shared the gruesome story and details.

Hearing how they had to screw the metal cage to his skull to hold his head still was appalling. It made me cringe to know that he was awake to watch a needle slowly approach his eyeball, only to be inserted multiple times to numb the eye. I was relieved to hear the final step of the radiation being used to dissolve the tumor. Chris's retell of it was like the script from a horror movie.

His eye healed well. Chris and the kids joked about designing eye patches and advertising them as fashion eyewear. I knew we would be able to heal physically and emotionally from this through the grace of God. With each visit, Chris encouraged his doctor to catch a good sermon and shared that he expected a full recovery in the eye. His doctor responds that his expectation is impossible and that it is highly unlikely to ever see anything but blackness.

At one of the appointments, a diagnostic image of the eye was taken to observe the eye's status. Upon the image was a visible marking. To Chris and his sister's amazement, they identify it as a cross. The symbol was not drawn on the picture by any hospital staff and was simply part of Chris's eye. The doctor and the staff attributed the marking to a blood vessel that burst or that it was the result of healing in the eye. However, our family recognized it as a sign of a cross, a sign from God of his protection and healing. As time goes by, vision, even though blurred and foggy, has improved in the eye. Chris jokingly states that he can even drive with it and claims that he would like to attempt it. We can only hope that he is only kidding about trying it out!

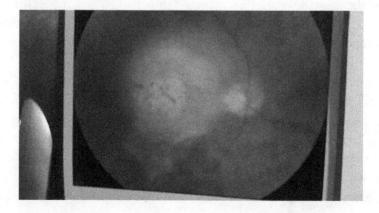

Hiatus

Two years after our bank nightmare started, our house was eventually placed on a website as a pre-foreclosure. The posting of our home created a dangerous situation and atmosphere for us. Having individuals drive by, park on the land, walk around the property, and take pictures of the house made it a tumultuous and challenging time.

One night, as our family was watching TV, Soleil suddenly screamed and pointed toward a window. A person interested in purchasing the property looked through the windows and attempted to get in to look around. The individual claimed that he thought the house was vacant, which was an unlikely story because our cars were in the driveway. Acknowledging the boldness of these property "vultures" and the impact that the bank's erroneous actions were having on the children meant we needed to act. Enough was enough!

We decided it was time to leave the property. So we started looking through the classifieds, looking for places to rent. In the local advertising magazine, I found a listing for a colonial. It was in town. It had four bedrooms. It was perfect but was a bit pricey; the rent was more than our mortgage, but what else could we do? We called and made an appointment to meet with the owner. We loaded up the car and drove to the house, which ended up being less than a mile away from our home.

As we approached the house, Chris exclaimed, "It's yellow! Does it have a crooked chimney?" He raced around the house to look at it.

Puzzled, I looked at him and asked, "What's going on?" He informed me that he had a dream of sorts where he believed God showed him a yellow colonial with a crooked chimney, and he felt at peace there. He thought it was God's way of telling him that is where we were meant to be.

Here we stood in front of a yellow colonial. It was exactly what our family needed. Across the street was a boy the same age as Sam named Dylan. The yellow colonial had four bedrooms and an inground pool. It was ideal. Unsure whether we were making the right decision, we felt comforted by the representative showing the house. She was friendly and welcoming. Upon hearing her last name, Blessings, we immediately knew that God had brought this place to us. So we signed a lease agreement and moved our family. However, we continued to send in documents and paperwork to the mortgage company to help identify their error and rectify the issue. This yellow house was lovely and what we needed, but it wasn't ours. And it wasn't home!

During our time at this house, Chris continued to struggle with health issues. He was now sleepwalking and sleep talking. Being in a new home with a second floor was dangerous. The family was abruptly awakened to a banging noise. As I jumped out of bed, I found that Chris wasn't in it. I ran to the staircase and found Chris in a ball at the end of the stairs. He was sleepwalking and fell down the stairs sound asleep. The ambulance was called, and he was brought to the hospital to be evaluated. From that moment on, we had to prop up children's safety gates all over the house for Chris's protection.

Chris's health and medical problems continued to build. He was diagnosed with sleep apnea. We decided that it was safer at the moment for Chris to sleep on the sofa on the first floor. It was not ideal, but it was safer for him. One day at work, I received a call from our neighbor Lori, informing me that she was with Chris at the bus stop, waiting for the school bus, and that he was not looking good. He asked her to call me, and so she did as asked and also called 911.

Through God's grace, we were fortunate that this neighbor was a nurse; she monitored his vitals and stayed with him until the ambulance arrived. She also ran into our house and was able to find the list of medications on the refrigerator and provided the list to the EMTs. Chris was fortunate to have her assistance that day, and we were grateful to be able to call her friend. Later we were informed that they believed that he suffered another TIA.

Besides the few hospital visits, our time at the yellow colonial was relatively peaceful. The kids especially enjoyed the pool. We were lucky to enjoy the pool for two fun-filled summers. A family campout with tents and late-night swims in the pool with built-in lights. Campfires, hotdogs, and s'mores made the weekends enjoyable. Sam seemed to grow up while we lived there. He learned how to ride a bike, first with training wheels and then without. Lori allowed Chris and the kids to drive the golf cart and our go-carts on her field. We had found a place of peace.

Home Again

Nearly two more years passed by. September arrives, and we receive some optimistic news. After writing a dispute letter and plea for help to the owner of the note, the attorney general, and Massachusetts's senator, we were contacted by a VP of the bank. She directed us to move back to the house and—if we had the documentation that we state we have—send it to her, and she would fix the problem.

So we did. This bank employee instructed us to return to the house; it needed to be immediate. While living at the other house we continued to monitor our home and were aware of the damage that the bank's property management company had done to the property. When we left the house, we had responsibly winterized the house to protect the new heating system installed during the renovations.

While we were out of the house, the banks' representatives turned on the water filling the pipes and, with no heat in the house, left parts of the house with damaged pipes. While doing so, they drove on our septic system, possibly damaging the cones in the design, presenting drainage and operation problems in the future. Moreover, since we still had hopes that this error would be fixed, we had left many items behind. However, the property management company looted the house, stealing anything that they could take out of the house.

With optimism that we were finally going to resolve this and move on, we followed her direction. We fixed the damage, replacing as much as we could to make it habitable for our family. The heating system was not reliable, working one day and not the next. What have we done? What about that dream of the yellow colonial with the crooked chimney? Were we meant to stay?

As the cold weather approached, we continued to question whether we had made a mistake in returning to our home. Our friend Wes once again came to our rescue. He delivered a woodburning stove; it was a lifesaver that provided heat for our family during the frigid winter. It was a long winter, many days questioning our decision to return and resume the fight.

*****

The summer finally came! Anyone who mocks teachers about having summer vacation needs to teach for 180 days. Summers are a time that allows teachers to regroup. However, to Chris's dismay, I applied and was hired to work in a three-week ELL (English Language Learners) summer program. Chris felt terrible that I would be working, but the pay came in handy. The program was half a day and four days during the week. It was perfect. The students and the families were always so grateful. Each day watching them walk their children to the door with smiles and hellos made it all worthwhile. That is why I became a teacher. It was work, but it also was my way to regroup and reset.

The afternoons and evenings were mine though! Chris created a private space for me right outside of the back door. A cement pad with a picnic table and a grill for our family dinners and a fire pit. I spent most of the summer nights sitting by the fire, listening and dancing to music. It was my heaven. Chris always had the fire pit prepped and ready to go.

One evening, as the embers slowly burned, it was time to call it a night. Before bed, Chris went out for one last check on the fire to ensure it was safe to let it slowly burn out. All of a sudden, he ran into the bedroom, grabbed his phone, and then back out. He eventually came back and turned on the light and asked, "Look at this! What do you see?" as he moves his phone up to my face. Begrudgingly, I take his phone and adjust my eyes in an attempt to see the image on the phone. "Do you see it?" he impatiently asks. "What do you see?" It was in the embers of the fire pit.

To my surprise, the image became clearer as my eyes focused. In the photo of the burning coals in the fire pit, my eyes were drawn to the symbol of a cross, which is what drew Chris's attention initially. But with closer scrutiny of the photograph, there appeared a semblance of the Virgin Mary holding Baby Jesus. Hearing this story, I know that others would probably consider us crazy, but as the expression states, "a picture is worth a thousand words."

Days later, I read an article: biblical signs in the sky on September 23, 2017—the same day that Chris took his picture of the embers. The article restated that on September 23, 2017, that an arrangement of celestial bodies occurred. It was written that "a great sign appeared in the sky, a woman clothed with the sun, with the moon under her feet and on her head a crown of twelve stars. She was with child…"

There are certain times that I truly feel that Chris is blessed and is being watched over. He strengthens my faith each day when I hear him ask others about their faith, encouraging them to catch a sermon; when he ends his goodbyes to the gas attendant with "Take care and God bless"; or when he leads our family in prayer before our meals! His faith and love are the qualities that brought us together, and it is times like these that I appreciate each day with him.

Sorry, Chris!

It was January, and this was a big year for both the boys. Zachary was going to be confirmed, and Samuel was receiving First Holy Communion. Both are special celebrations in the Catholic religion. The masses were about a month or so apart. We decided to celebrate both at the same time. Having one party would make things easier for family and friends attending and be financially more manageable. So if people were coming to the house, that meant we had to get the house ready.

When we moved back into our home, we cleaned and disinfected it to resume inhabiting it. But it was not guest-appropriate. We needed to address some home improvement projects to fix the damages created by the bank's property management company because they were eyesores. So we started painting. Everything looks better with a fresh coat of paint.

During February vacation, we were painting the foyer. Chris got a call on his cellphone. I didn't know who it was, but by the confused look on Chris's face, I had a feeling that it was not a social call. I continued painting in an attempt to finish the job as quickly as I could. There was still so much to be done. The party was less than a month away.

I looked around and noticed that Chris was no longer painting. The radio was blaring—helping to keep us working—was perhaps too loud for Chris, and he needed to find a quieter place to finish his phone call. Not thinking anything about it, I resumed painting and cleaned up. I was now feeling a bit miffed because I was left to clean up by myself. In my opinion, there is nothing worse than cleaning paint brushes and painting supplies.

Once I had cleaned up, I now found myself getting quite aggravated. "Where in the world did Chris disappear to? Nice of him to leave me with all the cleanup!" I searched all around the house. No Chris. I ask the kids, shrugging shoulder replies of *I don't know*. At this point, the aggravation was turning into anger. I finally found him. He was sitting in his car, still on the phone. I believe you could see the steam coming out of my ears as I walked closer to the vehicle. He puts up his pointer finger, indicating that he needed a minute. I stomped back into the house. Furious!

Eventually, Chris comes into the house. The kids and I are watching TV, trying to unwind from the day. Chris breezes by and doesn't respond when I ask who was on the phone. He retreated to our room, so I followed him. I will admit that I was ready for a confrontation; I was heated. How inconsiderate of him to leave me with all the cleanup. "So who was that? What was so important that you couldn't talk another time?"

As I began my barrage of questions, I quickly realized that something was wrong. His demeanor and expression was one that I haven't seen before. Looking defeated, he begins with, "I didn't want to talk to you in front of the kids. That call was the nurse from the doctors' office. She said that my blood work came back and that it didn't look good. They have scheduled an appointment with a nephrologist." I am blindsided. "What does that mean? What is a nephrologist? I don't understand!"

Chris was looking at me but appeared like he was looking through me, not quite grasping the information. He tells me, "I asked the nurse what that all meant, and all she said to me was, 'You will have to talk to the doctor about that. I'm sorry, Chris.' What does that mean, 'Sorry, Chris'?" he asks. He searches my face, appealing for support. I'm shell-shocked! I'm not sure what to say, trying to find the right words to reassure him. "Let's call your sister," I suggested. She was a retired RN and might be able to help us understand.

"I already did! She explained to me that a nephrologist is a kidney doctor. That's all that she could tell me." That response was another blow. "So you got this information, and instead of telling me, you called her first?" Hurt that he didn't confide in me first and worried about what we were to find out. Any good news doesn't end with "Sorry, Chris!"

Still unclear as to what that kind of doctor does, or generally what to expect, left us quite uneasy. Well, we went to the appointment with the nephrologist later that week. He introduced himself and went over the medical background. Then he addressed the elephant in the room: Chris was now in stage 4 kidney disease. He had cysts on both his kidneys. The damage was due to the prescribed medication that he took to address his diagnosed mood disorder. The nephrologist told us that the drug that he had been taking was notorious for damaging the kidneys.

I guess the news' severity didn't hit us because a close family member had just experienced a very close call due to a damaged liver. With help, time, and healthy changes, he was recovering. His liver was healing. So I think we naively thought the kidney was the same.

We were not sure how to respond when the doctor clarified that the kidney would never recover. He informed us that the goal was to keep the current kidney function level for as long as possible. The doctor's meeting was not optimistic, but we were reassured that the damage could be slowed down with changes. Many lifestyle changes needed to be made. Chris needed to start following a renal diet, which is a kidney-friendly diet. He also needed to increase his activity to help him lose weight. Finally, the biggest and the most important change was he needed to stop smoking. This change presented the hardest challenge for him, with many attempts ending in failure. Only with God's support and through prayer and determination was Chris finally able to conquer his addiction to nicotine.

Upon leaving, the office informed us that we had another appointment in two days with another department. The dialysis department! Still wielding from all the information, we left that appointment still somewhat determined to look on the brighter side. But then the dialysis informational appointment came. The friendly nurse introduced herself to us and escorted us to a room. We sat down, I set out my notebook and pen, and we prepared for the presentation. She expertly set up the TV and turned on the DVD. She informed us that she would be back once the video was complete and would answer any further questions—the video covered all the information, the types of dialysis, and the treatments' benefits. Interviews of patients ended the video explaining how dialysis helped improve their lives.

I find myself sitting there trying to be strong once again. I find it hard to swallow, my hands sweating, and I'm determined not to show my worry to Chris. I am usually the one taking notes and asking questions. As I look over at my husband, I see a tear roll down his cheek. I look away, my eyes well up, and I blink furiously, trying to hide my worry from Chris. I have only seen him cry one other time: the time his mother passed away. I didn't know what to say. I sat there hoping that he did not sense my worry.

We continued to sit there holding hands in silence. The nurse showed us around the clinic and asked if we had any questions. The reality of Chris's health condition had finally hit us. Still pretty solemn, we walked out of the office toward the car. Chris looked at me and said, "Well, that sucks!"

*****

Months went by, waiting and watching Chris as his blood work numbers dipped lower and lower. His energy level was slowly dissipating, and the physical and emotional effects of his failing kidneys were painfully obvious.

It was a difficult time for the family because even the family dinners were impacted. Dinnertime was a time to catch up and share the day's events. The effects of the kidney damage made eating an obligatory event, not an enjoyable one. Food no longer tasted good, and very often during or after dinner, Chris was nauseous or would be physically ill. At one of the doctor appointments, he was told that he had been put on the donation list. The doctor shared that there were different types of donations: donations from deceased individuals and living donors. The doctors informed us that if he were to receive a kidney donation, it would be best to try to hold off with dialysis for as long as possible. We were told that dialysis affected the body in ways that could impact the longevity of the kidney.

The time for Chris to start dialysis was inching closer and closer. His determination to wait and not start dialysis was commendable. However, the hammer dropped again. The transplant team decided to take Chris off the transplant list because of the previous eye tumor. Everything once again crashing down around us. How is this possible? Not sure how to proceed, it was a dim time for our family.

*****

Not sure what the future held for us, so we decided to renew our vows. Strange, you say; yes, it was! Years of turmoil, arguments, marriage counseling appointments, and threats of divorce. But we were still standing; we had made it through it all together, so why not? Worried about the future and whether Chris would be well enough or, God forbid, anything worse, we decided to renew our vows. Instead of waiting to celebrate the traditional twenty-fifth wedding anniversary, we decided to celebrate our twenty-third. Convincing Chris was the easy part. Now it was time to plan. We quickly realized and admitted that we would not be able to afford the kind of party we would have liked.

God certainly supported our plans because the church's pastor, our friend, offered us the use of the church gathering hall. It was in the basement of the adjoining church building. The hall was not glamorous, with dark brown paneling covering the walls, but it was perfect at the same time. After the church's blessing, the guests could walk across the parking lot and arrive at the reception. The hall had tables, chairs, bathrooms, and a kitchen. What else did we need? We planned a lovely event: the menu, an Italian buffet secured by hiring the local caterer, and I would bake and decorate cupcakes for dessert. My mom thought of all the decorating details, adding the last-minute touches, including the Mr. and Mrs. accents. We decorated the hall with twinkling Christmas lights, white and black tablecloths with pink accents.

We decided on a Friday night in May, and I worked that day. I thought it better to take a couple of days off following the party. A little getaway was planned for us to visit Chris's sister in Long Island for the weekend. Not having the day off to help with preparations was a big mistake. It ended up being a rainy night, and the caterer ran late. My parents were responsible for picking up the flowers and getting things ready in the hall, not enough hands to get everything prepared in a short amount of time.

Everyone in the church was waiting for me. Waiting to get the caterers set and running around in heels was a sight to see. Finally, Zachary came to the hall and informed me that I "better get to the church now. Everyone is waiting, and Dad is getting mad." So I reluctantly started walking in the rain to the church. To my relief, the caterer van pulled into the church parking lot. The food had arrived. I showed them where to set up and made my way to the church.

I looked in the church to see our family and friends sprinkled among the pews. A Bluetooth speaker quietly sent waves of the play-list's music, that the kids had thoughtfully created, across the church.

The kids led the way down the aisle. I am astonished at how beautiful the church looked in the evening, candles glittering and the sunset gleaming through the stained glass windows. It was a beautiful ceremony, and we all happily meandered over to the hall.

At this point, with the hall's lights dimmed, it was transformed into an intimate gathering place lit by the white Christmas lights. After dinner and toasts, the food tables moved to make room for a quaint dance floor.

One of Soleil's classmates agreed to be the night's DJ. As we did at our wedding, we decided to dance to a montage of songs; though this time, our kids were included. It was fun and set the stage for everyone to relax and enjoy, which—in my opinion—everyone did. Our guests enjoyed the food, music, and fun. You could hear the laughter coming from the photo booth that we set up off to one corner. It was a lovely night—an event that I will never forget, and one that I am so grateful was able to happen with the help and generosity of many.

Foreclosure Sale

The bank had scheduled another foreclosure sale on January 12. This was the third one scheduled, but it appeared that unlike the others that had been canceled, this one was going to happen. Each of the other sales were canceled before the actual day. It was just another way for the bank to harass us. The previous sales were published in the newspaper, but not the cancelation, which entailed being tortured by investors interested in the property still showing up and walking around our home.

However, by all indications, this sale was on. So I took the day out of work. It worked out because we had also planned to bring Sam to a swim meet in Boston. Sam was swimming for the YMCA team that Soleil was coaching at the time. We had planned to head up to Boston, enjoy a Friday in the city, have dinner, and stay overnight in a hotel, which sounded like a nice distraction. We sent Sam to school that day so that he would not witness any of the events at the house.

This sale was happening. People started to arrive at the house to look over the property and perhaps prepare themselves to bid during the auction. The past week, we had been blessed with a snowstorm. The height of the snow mounds on the sidewalks impeded the individuals attending the auction from parking in front of the house or along the sidewalk bordering the property. Cars continued to arrive and line our street. It was almost like God was crying along with us because it was a gray, rainy day.

We stood looking out the windows, watching people walk up and down the street looking at our home like we were an exhibition at the zoo. Watching and wondering how this was possible, poor Soleil decided to go out and videotape the individuals who had gathered like vultures ready to feed.

Individuals were angered by her, taunting her with comments like, "You should have paid your mortgage. We have a right to be here, deadbeat." It infuriated me to know that my daughter was being mocked. The anger helped me to set aside my grief. The sadness that this was really happening made me feel like I was going to be physically sick, but I was embarrassed and didn't want my daughter to see me like that.

As cars added to the congestion in front of my house, I called the police. I requested that those who were blocking my driveway be asked to move. We could not stop this injustice. I couldn't protect my family from this. An officer responded. I loudly shared the situation with him, projecting my voice so those people ready to take advantage of our plight could hear. Not that it made a difference because the individuals were simply there to make a profit.

The possibility to obtain a property for under its market value and the prospect of a payday was their incentive. They were not fazed by the fact that my family's home was being stolen from us. The almighty dollar and greed were all that they were concerned with. The sympathetic look on the police officer's face informed me that he couldn't do much, but he did have individuals move.

The auctioneer arrived on time and started to check people in. We held up the auction for as long as we could. No one got close to what the bank wanted. So the bank retained the property and, in their legal perspective, were now the legal owners. We gathered our overnight bags and eventually started our drive to Boston. It was hard to plaster that usual smile on my face, but it wasn't fair to Sam. It wasn't fair for Soleil or Zachary, for that matter, to share our worry or sadness. We all drove to Boston and had dinner. I guess I couldn't have planned a better distraction. Samuel was thrilled.

We had a wonderful meal at the hotel restaurant. Sitting with the family, enjoying some food and some quiet time, was what our family needed. Having the kids laugh at me as I lost my breath at the spice level of my ramen dish and watching as Sam marveled at the indoor glass elevators in the hotel was a blessing.

The next day, we proudly watched as Sam swam and Soleil guided her swimmers during the swim meet. Little did they know how defeated their parents felt on the inside.

Full Speed Ahead

February was a difficult month for me. I ended up having the flu and then pneumonia. I was quarantined in the back room so that I would not infect anyone else in the family. One Sunday, as I rested in my space, I heard a commotion. An individual knocked at the door and was determined to come into the house. He represented himself as a bank representative; he stated that he needed to get in and take pictures and document who was living in the house. Only when Chris asked for an ID and informed him that he would be calling the police if he remained did he finally leave.

The next day, we received a call from the new property management company. She called asking our intentions and offering money if we would voluntarily leave within the next seventy-two hours. I communicated to her that she should be contacting our attorney, that we had a case waiting to be heard in the courts, and that we had no intention of leaving until our case was heard in court.

Occupancy Notice

Ownership of the property, which you are currently occupying, has been transferred as a result of foreclosure proceedings.

You Have 48 Hours To Respond
To This Notice

Please contact

If We Do Not Hear From You We Will Assume That The Property Is Vacant And Will Change The Locks.

Please Contact Our Office Immediately.

That Wednesday, two days later, an employee of that same company came to the property to deliver a notice of eviction and take video and pictures of the property. This rude, insensitive person tossed the notice at Chris and asked for all the information that I provided to the company personally two days earlier. The notice now ordered us to vacate the house in seventy-two hours. This action was harassment.

I called the lady back at the company, and she denied any involvement. I informed her that we had pictures and the paper notice. She was curt, actually rude, and was not fazed by my complaint. I decided to go to the police department to document current events. Still battling pneumonia, I drove through the snow and rain to the police department. I was informed by the police officer that there was nothing that could be done unless they physically caught them trespassing.

The next day, we informed our attorney of the events. He called the management company, advocating for us in an attempt to end the harassment, while we waited for our day in court. However, following the foreclosure sale, we renewed our campaign to bring attention to our situation. The following week was winter vacation; feeling better, I drafted a letter about our situation. The letter summarized our desperation and our determination to fight for our due process of law. The email asked for help, and I was hoping that the correspondence would bring attention to our plight. I worked on emailing our letter to every senator and member of congress in the United States; I also emailed it to the US president again, to some newspapers, and a few famous Hollywood personalities known to assist those in need. The following text is the letter that we sent out appealing for assistance.

The letter read: *Are all men created equal? Are they endowed by the Creator with certain unalienable rights, that among these are life, liberty, and the pursuit of happiness? It is our understanding that "the Constitution makes no distinction as to the wealth or status of persons; all are equal before the law, and all are equally subject to judgment and punishment when they violate the law. The same holds true for civil disputes, involving property, legal agreements, and business arrangements. Open access to the courts is one of the vital guarantees written into the Bill of Rights."*

In 2009, due to a bank error, our mortgage was placed into foreclosure. Since November 2009, we have been trying tirelessly to correct this mistake by talking to numerous bank representatives and departments and submitting documents over and over again, hiring multiple attorneys, and appealing for assistance from state representations and departments. We have endured a nightmare but continued to try to rectify the mistake. We have acted in good faith and met all the bank's requests and demands, including moving out and back into the property and fixing damage to the property caused by the bank's property management company, and the list goes on. Our mortgage has been shuffled three times, allowing no resolution on the bank's part and compounding our problem. A foreclosure sale was held even though our case is currently waiting to be heard in the courts.

It has come to our attention that, due to the 2009 housing crisis, there are many cases being submitted to the courts. Whether intentional or not on the bank's part, the courts are being flooded by foreclosure cases. Being faced with the sheer numbers of the cases being submitted by the banks, many are being consolidated and not seen on a case-to-case basis. Not all foreclosure cases are alike and should be read and tried fairly.

We are not writing for financial help. We are asking that you help bring public awareness of this problem. In essence, we are writing for your assistance to help us and others who have been wronged by the banks to ensure that we receive our due process of law. Please help!

I was amazed to hear back from a senator. I wasn't even a constituent of this politician, but he responded! It was promising that he replied; he responded multiple times and appealed to the attorney general for us. Someone finally heard me! Not sure if it would do anything, but I felt comforted that someone acknowledged our problem.

The office of this senator contacted me three times, providing suggestions and offering their sympathy to our family for our nightmare. At this point, school's winter break was over, and I was back to work. It just happened that I found out that our school was scheduled to be visited by one of the state's congressmen. He was going to read a book to all the second grade. I couldn't believe it!

I printed out our letter, and before he left, I politely approached him. Politely reaching out to him, I show him the envelope. I introduced myself and pleaded that he take a few minutes to read my family's story on his way back to his office. He graciously accepted the envelope and reassured me that he would read it. I thanked him for my family and me and continued my day, teaching with a hopeful heart.

The congressman did honor his word. He must have read the letter because we received a call from his office. The office had reached out to the attorney general's office in an attempt to assist us. We are notified that the attorney general could not do anything since the case is in the courts. No surprise! The former AGO and current Massachusetts senator did nothing to help. They contacted the bank; the bank reported that all was accounted for, and they took their word for it. The banks are like the all-powerful Oz behind the curtain, like in the story *The Wizard of Oz*. No one questioned. The bank and its lobbyists have so much power.

It had come to our attention that the courts have a negative view of the homeowners. We are seen as the problems in the court. How can we fight for our rights when the courts look at us as troublemakers? Not all foreclosures are due to people taking mortgages that they can't afford. We put a substantial down payment on this house when we purchased it, had added on additions through the years, and made the monthly payments that the bank was now claiming were never paid. In our case, we were placed into foreclosure status wrongly.

Payments were made and accepted by the bank, and they were denying receipt of them. Not sure where our payments went, who got it, but I know the bank took our money, and our bank statements prove it, the money was withdrawn from our account by them. Having no control of the situation that the bank put us in, having to confront the fact that the bank was being allowed to steal my home was infuriating! I don't think there is anyone that can understand this abuse, this violation. It was beyond financial. Once again, we had put everything into the house—our money, sweat labor, heart, and soul.

Our attorney continued to fight for us. He informed us that a judge had now stepped down, declaring that he had financial interests regarding one of the top bank cases. This situation provided us with a moment to breathe and contemplate the possibility that we would be validated. However, the reprieve was short-lived.

In reviewing recent judgments, we learned that not only did the courts dismiss any possible financial influence on judgments made by this judge, but they were also now fining homeowners and fining them for continuing frivolous cases in their opinion. I found myself screaming, "Frivolous! It's not the homeowners. It's the banks with the deep, endless pockets continuing and postponing cases." Hearing how other cases were proceeding and how other homeowners were struggling as we were was a devastating reality. Now aware that the courts were penalizing homeowners who have attempted to fight for their rights was another hard pill to swallow.

Unable to accept the injustice, I found it unfathomable that my home could be taken from us. Determined that we were right, we were justified to fight. But realistically, Chris was starting to wonder if we should finally succumb to the strength of the all-powerful banks. It was not fair; I found myself sobbing and asking, *Why? Why can our government, our courts, our society allow for such mistreatment?* It appeared to me that the theft of a citizen's property was approved, accepted, and rewarded because of the banks' greed and their representatives.

We Found Her!

From the time Chris had found out that he was adopted, he wanted to search for his birth parents. He did not pursue the search while his adopted mother was alive. Even though he was curious, he did not want to cause her any hurt or pain. The search was not to replace her but to learn more about himself and where he came from.

Since it was years since his mom had passed away, Chris had signed up on a registry. The registry was a list of names and their identifying information; information such as place of birth and birthdate. Once on the list, if birth parents searched and provided the same information, both parties would be notified. Rhode Island was one of the remaining states that had closed adoptions. With Chris's health issues, he also tried to have a medical letter assist in opening his adoption file. Unfortunately, he was not successful. He would have to wait and hope that his birth parents would start a search.

The only information that he had was from the center that his birth mother had resided at during her pregnancy. In the information, some notation was written by the nursing staff that the family strongly supported adoption and that it was in the baby's best interest to be adopted by another family. In 1965, being a single unwed mother was not readily accepted. Hearing that Chris was still searching, his sister shared his story with her friend. Her friend ended up having an interest in researching lineage and was exceptionally talented in finding out information. She shared some information about signing up on a website that helped with adoption reunions.

As months passed, she was able to find newspaper clippings and finally was able to say, "We found her!" Eventually, both his sister and the "detective" were positive that they had located Chris's family. His sister worked up enough courage and called the suspected family member, and she left a voice message. A few days later, Chris's sister received a call, and the unfamiliar phone number gave suspect that it was the person she had left that voice message with earlier. After a nervous hello and tentative pause, she conveyed to his sister her excitement to have been contacted. The research paid off, and it was Chris's biological aunt. Unfortunately, his birth mother had passed away, but at least he now had a connection.

After some correspondence between his sister and his biological aunt were shared, Chris reached out to her himself. His aunt shared some stories and some pictures of his mom with Chris. He was disappointed to have not met his mom but was grateful to hear some of the stories about her.

We learned through an email correspondence that she and her husband would be visiting family on Martha's Vineyard. A meeting was planned and scheduled. Chris and the family would be able to meet her and her husband.

As the date approached, the weather seemed to once again mirror our excitement and nervousness. A hurricane hit New England. Ferries were canceled, and it was not looking like the meeting was going to happen. On the day of the meeting, we drove to the ferry and waited in a long line. It was cold and raining. Pushed and bumped by unhappy vacationers trying to get to the island for reservations; everyone was trying to get on the ferry. Due to the conditions, only the larger ferries were running, so people anxiously tried to get on the limited runs. We were able to get tickets. Numbers were taken, and each person counted as they boarded the ferry. I'm not sure how they did it, but every seat was filled with some standing. We all identified where the life preservers were if there was boat trouble.

Sitting at a table made to seat six comfortably, the five of us squished with three other people and endured the choppy ride to the island. In true Chris fashion, he struck up a conversation with the family sitting with us. It would have been an awkward ride if he had not, since we were sitting so close. As he told the story, the family listened intently. It helped to pass the time.

Finally, we reached the island. As we docked, we started our search for his aunt. The blustery day certainly made finding them difficult. Chris received a text from his aunt sharing their location and that they were in a minivan. We were able to find them; we all run through the rain, cramming into the minivan made for a rushed encounter. Quick introductions were made, and handshakes were exchanged.

Reservations were made at a nearby restaurant, and it was great to warm up and have a chance to chat. His aunt and uncle were gracious and forthcoming. Chris sat on the edge of his chair, listening to his aunt's stories about his mom. Many of the stories involved an interest of cars and being free spirits made it clear that Chris and his biological mother were kindred spirits.

Chris and the family shared stories and gave his aunt an album of pictures of Chris and the family. We had lunch, and due to the weather, we thought it best to take a ferry home sooner than later. It would not have been wise to press our luck and be stranded on the island. We said our goodbyes and boarded the ferry. The sea was still rough, but the ride home was comforting. It was nice to have met her, and it was a memorable meeting, one that none of us will ever forget.

Social Media

Meanwhile, during our continued fight with the banks, Chris's health had continued to decline. His kidney function was at the point where he should start to consider starting dialysis. His skin color was now a grayish tint. He hardly had any energy and was drinking way too much coffee, which was not good for him, but he was always tired. His moods were variable, and he lost track of his thoughts.

Chris still stubbornly refused to start dialysis. Fortunately, he was given miraculous news. With the help of his eye doctor, he was cleared to return to the donation list. His type of eye tumor, as the doctor explained, was not a type that would return. That was documented by the data collected from the doctor appointments following the gamma knife procedure. It was now a waiting game. But was he going to make it long enough to get to the top of the list? Would a match ever be found?

His sisters were determined to help. They wanted to help but how? It was decided that a Facebook page would be created and that we appeal to social media. A letter about Chris, his family, and his appeal for a living kidney donor was posted. We were encouraged, as it is shared and liked. Amazingly, several people responded and called the transplant clinic inquiring about being tested.

One individual who stepped up was chosen to be evaluated. He was around the same age as Chris and enthusiastically started testing. How uplifting it was to learn that there was hope. This gentleman was informed that he was a match. Wow! He shared his progress with my sister-in-law regarding parts of the evaluation. This actually might happen; Chris remained hopeful and grateful but knew that it was still only a possibility.

The devastating news came that during the evaluations this individual was denied as a possible donor. It was so disappointing, but this man was so gracious and apologetic. We were so thankful for his courage and for stepping up and attempting to be a donor. Following that news, another individual who inquired about donating was called. This person read Chris's story and was touched. We all waited patiently for the results of the blood work. It felt like a lifetime. Eventually, we heard there was another match. This time we all tried to be a bit more reserved in our optimism. But behind the scenes, many candles were being lit, and prayers being said.

Chris was working hard at keeping his kidney function from declining any further. We visited a nutritionist and found diets and food preparations to help reduce his potassium and phosphorus intake. Months passed, and the donor would send messages of encouragement to Chris's sister, informing us that testing was going well, and no roadblocks as of yet.

As usual, during one of Chris's appointments, we sat in the exam room waiting for the doctor, discussing our questions, and preparing ourselves for any possible curveballs. As his nephrologist entered, he looked at the file; he flipped through the pages as usual. He reviewed the recent tests and blood work. My heart dropped as he sat down. My mind was racing. *What could he be bracing us for now? What's wrong?*

He slowly closed the folder, placed it on the counter behind him, and said, "Well, the donor was approved, and it is a go." What a miracle! First of all, to find another donor that was a match and to have the donor approved were a blessing from God. Before we had a chance to celebrate, he cautioned us not to get too excited. He had participated in a couple of surgeries in which the donor backed out. "There are no promises. The donor can back out at any time." We couldn't believe our ears. Is this going to happen?

This person must be an amazing individual. It was surreal! Learning about the damage that Chris's body was encountering and that, through this surgery, he would be allowed to live a fuller, longer life, I was so grateful to this generous, caring hero.

We learned that the surgery was to be set, but the donor wanted to remain anonymous for the moment. Amazing! It was mind-blowing to think that there was an individual out there that wanted to help a perfect stranger. The person didn't even want to be acknowledged or known for their selflessness, courage, and strength! I marveled at this person! How would I ever be able to communicate with this person their impact on our family and how grateful I am?

Summer Fun!

With the possibility of the surgery happening soon, Chris wanted to have some time with the family. We planned some activities that were close by. The first trip was to Old Orchard Beach. The five of us enjoyed some time sharing a suite in a hotel that we have visited before. We spent the time splashing in the heated pool, shopping on the pier, and enjoying the fruits of the ocean. It was luxurious! There is nothing better than fresh lobster dipped in butter, sweet steamer clams, and salty little necks. It was heaven, and our family certainly treasured the messy delicious meals.

A day trip to Canobie Lake Park was our next excursion. Samuel has never visited Disney World or any other large amusement parks, so this was planned with him in mind. The day was beautiful. We all enjoyed a boat ride around the lake, looking at all the properties that were built around the lake and dreaming and pointing at which of the houses we would like to own if we were ever to win the lottery. The kids enjoyed riding all the rides, and Sam discovered that he loves roller coasters. I think that the kids rode each ride at least three times each. Their smiles and laughter were just what the doctor ordered for Chris.

Eventually, the walking and excitement of the day took its toll on Chris. Exhausted but happy to watch the kids, he gratefully found shaded benches to rest on. Having our fill of the rides and sun, we called it a day and headed home.

Being encouraged that Chris handled all the day's walking at the amusement park, we decided to visit Purgatory Chasm. A state reservation was just a short drive away, and it would be a fun place for the kids to hike and explore the rocks and caves. It was an outside excursion, and we could have a picnic there. The weather was beautiful, and we headed out to enjoy a hike with the kids. It brought back memories because Chris had taken me there when we were dating.

Unfortunately, we went the day after a rainstorm, and my white converse sneakers were not made for hiking during that visit decades ago. I slipped and skinned up my knees. It was not something that I wanted to repeat, so we left climbing on the rocks strictly to the kids. Chris and I enjoyed a walk on the more-leveled terrain. In looking over the pictures, Chris's skin tone and his stamina were indicative of his illness. Thankful for another day together, but worried that his condition worsened with each day.

Set Your Calendar!

Finally, the date was set: Monday, September 24th! It was Chris's sister's birthday! What a blessing! Chris and I were called into the transplant clinic a couple of weeks before the operation to learn about post-transplant directions. The nurse went over what the schedule would look like. Details like when to arrive, where to go to check-in, and all the other aspects of the surgery day were explained.

Then there was an explanation of all the things to be careful and mindful of following the transplant. The teacher in me kicked in because the nurse informed us that there will be a literal quiz that was reviewed following the surgery before discharge. You need to know this stuff! It's a good thing too because I notice that Chris had a bewildered look on his face as I looked over. He had resorted to cracking jokes, and I had a feeling that all he heard at that moment was the Charlie Brown teacher's voice saying, "Blah, blah, blah!"

During the meeting, we inquired about the donor. We were informed that the donor was a woman and that she might be open to meeting on the surgery day. After some discussion, the team decided that the meeting would probably be best if conducted after the surgery. The nurse reassured us that if all went well and everyone was willing, something could be set up before discharge. So we all wait on pins and needles, hoping both Chris and the donor remain healthy. It's hard to describe the following two weeks. In one sense, it seemed like an eternity because I just wanted it to be over. I was so anxious that the donor would have second thoughts.

But then time seemed to fly by because there was so much to do. I had to get things ready for Chris, get things ready at the house, and make schedules for the kids about chores, responsibilities, and car pickup times for Sam when he had an after-school meeting for one of his clubs or band. Most importantly, I had to get sub plans ready for my leave. I had been granted family leave time to stay home and care for Chris. This was difficult for me; since it was September, I only had a couple of weeks with my new students.

The beginning months were so vital in establishing routines, and being a bit of a control freak regarding my classroom was another source of stress, to say the very least. However, I was fortunate enough to have the daughter of a colleague, who was a recent graduate with her teaching degree, agree to be placed into the long-term sub position. It was ideal. She was excited and enthusiastic. During our conversations, her demeanor was patient but firm; she was a godsend.

After some consideration, we permitted the kids to stay home from school on the day of the surgery. How could they possibly function at work, or be ready to learn? It was a miraculous day for Chris and our family and for his sister; it was her sixtieth birthday. So the kids invited her to join them at a mass that morning and then to a birthday breakfast. Many people, including his sister and my parents, asked about waiting with me at the hospital during the surgery. Chris's thoughts were that no one should stay and wait. He even wanted me to go home. I decided that I would stay. What would I do at home, worry? I might as well remain at the hospital so that I could see him when he got to recovery.

My teammates at work had given me a bag of hospital necessities. Magazines, snacks, lunch money, and an Alex and Ani mantra bracelet that had "She believed she could and she did." engraved on it. They gave it to me the Friday before the surgery.

As they handed me the bag and I opened the card, I was overwhelmed with emotion. I couldn't believe it. Here I am crying in front of my friends as they show me their love and support. How embarrassing! I have fine-tuned the ability of self-distraction so not to show weakness. The more I add to my to-do list, I am kept busy enough to not think about things. This to-do list governed my life to this point, and it helped me be devoid of showing my emotions. I am thankful for the family and friends that have been there to help me through this difficult time.

Surgery

Finally, the day of the surgery arrived. The alarm rang, and everyone got up. The kids hugged their dad. I kept busy, gathered the hospital bag, my bag of magazines, and snacks. It was time to head to the hospital. Our trip to the hospital was a quiet one. I kept reassuring myself silently everything is going to be okay. *Don't show him that you are worried. He needs you to be strong.*

So we parked in the parking garage and walked to the hospital. Dawn was approaching, and it was so quiet. The dark sky was slowly lighting up to start the day. We found our way to the registration office. We checked in, signed paperwork, and then took our seats, waiting to be called. Looking around, wondering if any of the women there were the donor. Chris was checked in and escorted to the pre-op area.

In true Chris fashion, he was making jokes and keeping the conversation light. He asked me to take a picture of him as he pulled the hairnet over his face. "Please send it to the kids and my sisters so they don't worry."

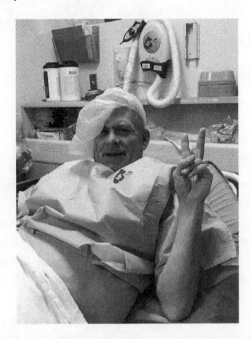

It was almost 8:00 a.m. at this point. We were in a small area with all curtains drawn, but we could hear the hospital staff's hustle and bustle, getting prepared for the day of surgeries ahead. We could hear the conversations of other patients as they awaited their surgeries. Once again wondering if his donor was close by. She could be in the section right next to us.

It was time for me to leave so that they could complete the next steps to get him ready for the surgery. I reached out to hug him, and he looked at me with his blue eyes. His gaze was a combination of worry and hope. "I love you. I'll be here waiting for you. It's going to be okay!" I say as I kiss him, and they escorted me out.

As I walked away, I looked back, and he held up the peace sign to reassure me. They brought me to the surgery waiting room and told me that I would be informed once Chris was out of surgery.

It was the longest day of my life. I believe I spent the morning reading my magazines, but I'm not sure. The TV was on, but I'm not sure what program was showing; I could hear the voices but didn't comprehend what was being said. The waiting room was dark, allowing those who had accompanied their loved ones for surgery to nap during their long wait.

Now almost noon, while I sat in the room, a person assigned to inform visitors about how the surgeries were going approached me. She handed me a card with numbers on it. The card had the tracking number for Chris's procedure, and I was able to check on the surgery's status by looking at the TV screen.

Hours passed by with the words "Surgery in Progress" posted next to Chris's numbers. Finally, around 1:00 p.m., I am told that the surgery is complete and that he is being moved to recovery. Another hour passes, and after my fifth attempt to see Chris, a nurse asked me to follow her. I ask about the donor, and the nurse tells me that she is awake, out of recovery, and has been moved to a room.

As I am led through the recovery area, I see Chris in the hospital bed with his eyes closed. I rub his arm and whisper, "Hey there. I'm here."

He slightly opened his eyes and asked, "How is the donor?" For a moment, I feel hurt that he doesn't acknowledge me. I've been downstairs waiting all this time, praying for him, stressed out. But eventually, it dawns on me that that's precisely why I love him. Not many people know Chris the way I do. He is a caring, sensitive man under that hard exterior. So what other question would he ask? This whole miracle is not about me but them.

3251729	Surgery in progress	
3251790	In Recovery	
3261617	Preparing to Leave Recovery	
3268839	Procedure or Surgery Complete	
3268914	Surgery in progress	
3268989	Procedure or Surgery	

After I updated him about the donor, he closed his eyes to rest. The nurses informed me that I need to return to the waiting room once again. Once he leaves recovery and is in a room, they will let me know—what a long day. Eventually, my parents drop off the kids; we have dinner together in the cafeteria. Once again, I am thankful to have food and time with my children. Their critiques of the cafeteria's pulled pork and mac and cheese helped to ground me. We were allowed to visit with Chris once he was settled.

The nurse was attending to him, the kids kissed him, and we went home. Relieved! Thankful! Exhausted!

*****

The following day was a blur. Doctors were visiting, nurses checking in on him, and Chris sleeping most of the day. Another long day of sitting in a hard recliner. Anyone who has spent any amount of time will attest to the discomfort of those chairs. With each hour that passed, I could feel my back clenching up and the stress of it all slowly building into a rheumatoid arthritis flare-up. Chris convinced me to go home with the kids and have a good night's rest.

I have to say that I did not argue and gratefully went home. My colleagues at work had dropped off meals for the kids and me. What a blessing! We ate a casserole of chicken marsala and had a chance to catch up on everyone else's day. I took a warm shower, and as I got ready for bed, I noticed that I missed a call on my cell phone; but it wasn't a number I recognized.

There was a voicemail left. The voice was not familiar at first. I replayed it, and to my horror, it was Chris. I was frightened by the message of "Thank you very much for answering your phone. I really needed you. I need you to come here!"

I called the hospital, and the nurses' desk was unable to give me any information. I finally got through to Chris's room. The panic and worry in his voice were disturbing. Quickly, Soleil and I get dressed and raced back to the hospital. Unfortunately, during the time that we went home, there were some issues. The catheter was not emptied and backed up, which could present a new kidney transplant with many problems.

Moreover, his medications were not given at the proper time. We were instructed many times of the importance of routine consistent administration, and the worry of it all put Chris in an emotional state. He felt unsafe and wanted to leave. He was yelling directives for us to call an ambulance and have him shipped to another hospital. "They are going to ruin this kidney. I'm in danger here. After all, this effort, it's all for nothing. I want to get out of here. I NEED to get out of here!"

The nurses and the staff were in defense mode, so the need to advocate for his pills, change of bedding and clothes, and discussion of the situation turned to Soleil and me. We were able to get his pills eventually. Having the pills eased us all a bit. Worries of rejection and still unsure of the transplant's success still hung heavy over all of us.

After some time, we were able to convince him to stay; and due to the turn of events, it made it necessary for me to stay with him. Due to the questions and concerns that had transpired, Chris demanded that I or someone else from the family stay with him during his time at the hospital.

Chris's sister graciously visited for lunch and would stay in the afternoon so that I would be home when Sam returned home from school. Having her stay with Chris gave me a chance to shower and take a nap. The hectic schedule and its stress all prevented me from sleeping, but it was nice to rest in my bed.

His sister was also able to meet with the donor at this time. They had shared correspondences during the testing period to see whether she was a match and able to donate. Our gifts of thanks were left for the donor on her nightstand. Flowers and a simple bracelet with the engraved message of "If God brings you to it, He will bring you through it." We hoped that the message would convey that we were praying for her for a smooth and quick recovery. We all were hoping to be able to meet the donor while she and Chris were recovering. The donor was doing so well that she was discharged early, and plans would have to be made to meet later.

No Place Like Home

Eventually, the time came for Chris's discharge. The day before was spent meeting with all of the specialists. First was the nurse who went over the "transplant bible." It included all the information that we needed to remember. Chris and I were required to complete a quiz of the information mentioned at the intake meeting when all this first was set in motion.

When the nurse started asking questions, Chris started making jokes, which irritated her. Obviously, he did not read the information; as a teacher, I would say that he did not read to comprehend, or that he did not do a deep read. That was my cue to step in and answer the questions to reassure the hospital staff that he would follow all the instructions.

Next came the nutritionist. It was another awkward meeting, sitting in the room with Chris and the nurse bantering back and forth about hospital protocol and procedures. Being trapped in his hospital room, Chris had heard and seen the nurses' plight since their recent union walkout. The terms of their new contracts and the hospital administration's greed had, as it often does, created a rift. Hospital equipment, working hours, and resources were not as the board of directors would have like outsiders to perceive. The forced laughs of the nurse and the blunt retort was not getting anyone anywhere. Through the grace of God, the meeting was over.

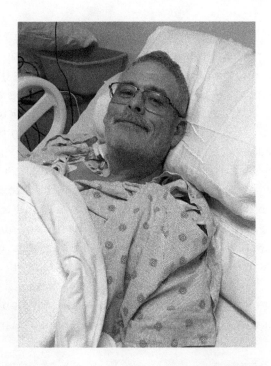

After lunch was time to fill the prescription case with the week's pills. The nurse instructed us to wash our hands and showed us how to open and set the bottles just so. When the pills were placed into the correct compartment, the bottle should be placed behind the cover so that it reminds you that the pill has already been included in the case. Both Chris and I were asked to take a separate bottle, read the label, count the pills, and place them in the case.

Each time verbally reminded to be mindful as to how to return the pill bottle. It seemed silly that everything had to be so particular but looking back; it was an effective and useful practice. With many more prescriptions added to his list, I find the routine reassuring, and I'm thankful for the nurse's absolute determination to have it done the right way!

The pharmacist visited next. Such a sweet and serious young girl. She was not deterred or affected by Chris's humor. She went over the list of prescriptions and explained what each of them did. I took notes and asked questions to be sure that we remembered all that was shared with us that day.

Last but not least, the transplant team stopped by. They all walk in as a group with their shiny white coats and stethoscopes dangling. Chris was reminding them to use the hand sanitizer as they entered. Some of the physicians were put out with eyes rolling and huffing sounds, but a smiling face and reassuring nodding doctor joins the group, stating, "Yes, you are doing what you were told to do, advocating for your safety. Hello, Mr. Marcotte."

That was Chris's nephrologist. He was then and continues to be a calming, honest voice of reason. Sharing the information and updates regarding his current blood work, vitals, and tests all indicated that he was ready to leave. They answered our questions and wished him well. The discharge papers were prepared. Once again, the nurse went over the discharge plans and scheduled a visiting nurse to check on Chris during the first few weeks at home. Chris was jumping out of his skin. He was not physically jumping, but it was apparent that he had had enough of the hospital. Time to go!

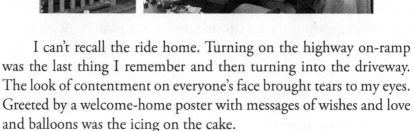

I can't recall the ride home. Turning on the highway on-ramp was the last thing I remember and then turning into the driveway. The look of contentment on everyone's face brought tears to my eyes. Greeted by a welcome-home poster with messages of wishes and love and balloons was the icing on the cake.

Something Is Just Not Right

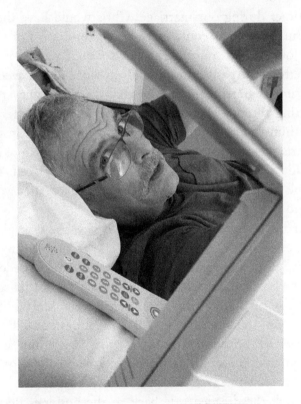

It was terrific having Chris home. Don't get me wrong; it was a lot of work. My days were consumed with driving him back to the hospital each day for the first week for blood work, giving him his pills three times a day, cooking his meals, taking and recording his vitals in our log three times a day, and making sure everything was sanitized.

Each day started very routinely. Pills were provided with his glass of water and his cup of black coffee as he sat in the TV room watching his favorite evangelist. Chris liked listening to this pastor because of his uplifting and relatable stories. The story of Job in the Bible is one that he refers to, and one for which Chris identifies with and takes comfort. "If Job could overcome, so can I." Many of Chris's trials and tribulations seemed to parallel those mentioned in the story of Job.

At times during our marriage, Chris would have these horrifying sulfur burps that could singe the eyebrows off of you. "See, just like Job. This is too much!" Chris would wallow in his misery. Thankfully the gastrointestinal disturbance would eventually go away, leaving us grateful and hoping that they would never return.

Starting the day after discharge, the nurse started visiting to check on him to ensure that he was following all the instructions. Later, Chris was not feeling well. His urine was not looking right, and he had pain over the location that Brutus was placed. Yes, Chris named the kidney Brutus, claiming that the organ was a tough fighter, and Brutus seemed appropriate.

After his blood work on the fourth day, the transplant clinic called. The results of the blood work showed something was not quite right. While I was gathering all the items that he needed to have while in the hospital, I started to break down. "Did I do something wrong? What if I did? What's going to happen? Maybe I shouldn't have given him the blueberry yogurt! Was it pasteurized?" I started looking over all the labels of the foods that I gave him and started mentally going over everything that I fed him and did during the few days that he was home.

We took the dreaded ride back to the hospital. Results indicated either rejection or infection. His creatine, the kidney function indicator in his blood test, was creeping up, and that was not a good sign. No matter the reason for the changes, the treatment was the same: days of heavy-duty antibiotics and steroids. Eventually, the blood work showed that his body and the kidney were responding. Everything was going to be okay. Phew!

*****

The following year ended up being a trying one: multiple trips back to the hospital. Days spent in the emergency room waiting for a room to open up on floor 6, the kidney floor—having no option but to go through the ER, which was the hospital's admission procedure. This procedure of not conducting a direct room admission presented many problems. It not only extended the time at the hospital but also meant creating more bills to be paid and other issues.

The most frustrating and frightening issue was the exposure to the other patients in the ER. Being surrounded by sick individuals with illnesses, germs, and viruses—everything that we worked so hard to keep away from him—made Chris feel very unsafe. Frequent arguments of "I'm safer at home. I want to go home. I shouldn't be here" did not help to move along the admittance process. It did have an impact though! Many times, he was flagged as argumentative, irrational. One time he even had a psych consult called on him because the doctor did not appreciate how he questioned her, and she felt he needed medication.

Since that night following the transplant, I accompanied Chris to each hospital visit, every doctor's appointment, and during each hospital stay. We found that having another individual hear the doctor's diagnosis and advocate for patient care was integral in Chris's health and well-being. Having me there to clarify or question medical actions gave Chris's concerns credibility.

The nursing staff became very familiar with Chris and me. Some of them were friendly and happy, as happy as someone is to see someone readmitted to the hospital. Others dreading his return with polite greetings of "Oh, hello again" as they quickly avert their attention to other issues. The doctors, the nurses, the nursing supervisors, the patient advocate department all got to know us quite well.

As in the education environment, it is vital to have all sides working together as a team. The hospital and the doctors have realized that Chris and I want to learn as much as possible and follow all the steps needed to keep Chris and Brutus healthy. I have become quite versed at reading the blood work reports on his portal and familiar with his medications and their dosage.

Medication updates and changes not recorded, sanitizing or lack thereof, and poor hospital conditions were all valid concerns that we communicated to all involved. The once quiet, timid, and shy girl has now been replaced with an inquisitive, determined advocate. I'm not sure when that happened, but when my family needs it, I will no longer sit by idly and allow anything other than they receive the best possible plan, care, or treatment, whether that be medical or otherwise.

Meeting an Angel

The December after the transplant, a meeting with the donor was set. Both she and Chris were doing well and were up for a gathering. During the time between the meeting and the transplant, we learned more about our hero. She was a single mom who ended up being the acquaintance of one of Chris's friends. She was touched by the story that was shared on Facebook. Something inside of her compelled her to help out, which we feel was the Lord's intervention.

For the meeting, we decided to keep the gathering small. We invited her and her family; our family; our mutual friend who inadvertently made it all possible; and Chris's sister, responsible for starting the social media campaign.

The house twinkled with Christmas lights, looking festive and welcoming. The time came. Unfortunately, due to prior commitments, her daughter was unable to join us. It was amazing to be sitting with this angel in my kitchen, not sure what to say or how to thank her. Immediately she started sharing how she was feeling, telling us about her and her family. She even bravely showed us her scar. Wow! What a phenomenal person.

The kids and I shared a poem written for her and presented her with a little angel necklace. She proudly waved her wrist, showing that she was wearing the bracelet that we gave to her on the transplant day, and at the same time reassuring us that the gifts were not needed. Our lovely night ended with thank-yous and hugs. We turned off the lights, reflecting on the evening's events and thanking God for bringing this spectacular, selfless individual into our lives.

*****

While writing about our family's angel, it is a nice transition to another incident that put a guardian angel to work. The older children were out with their friends. So we decided to order pizza and have a movie night with Samuel. It was a lovely, quiet, relaxing evening. Being a young thirteen-year-old, Samuel was still awake and not ready for bed. So he went to his room and joined some of his friends on his video games. It is amazing how gamers have the opportunity to connect virtually with others over the various gaming platforms. So far from Pong and Pac Man's games that kept us "gaming dinosaurs" occupied and entertained way back when.

Being one of those aforementioned dinosaurs, I was ready for bed early on a Saturday night. Soleil likes to mock us as we fall asleep during movie nights by commenting on how Chris and I are no longer "Ragers!" That being said, Chris and I retired for a good night's sleep.

Hours later, we are woken up by the sound of the cell phone's ring. At this point, it was past midnight, and the house was quiet. As Chris answered the phone, I heard a tone that scared me more than the actual words. It was Zachary, and I heard, "D-d-dad, I was in an accident, and it's bad. It's bad." I could hear the fear and anxiety of my son from across the king-size bed. His father jumped up to attention like I haven't seen in quite a few years. He grabbed on a pair of jogging pants, hopping into each of the legs like a participant in a potato sack race. With one hand holding the pants, the other hand holding his phone to his ear. He was so calm and matter-of-fact. So not like the typical Chris. He was methodically asking probing questions. "Where are you? Are you okay? Anyone with you? I'll be right there."

Zachary was in an accident on his best friend's road. He had just dropped his friend off, and on his way home, his right front tire came completely off. Once the tire fell off, the full-size SUV was immediately pulled to the right, crashing into two parked cars. His vehicle's weight plowed into one car, pushing that car into the car parked in front of it. It was a terrible accident. His GMC Denali and the two other vehicles were totaled.

Chris made it there at the same time that the police arrived. Having Chris there was a godsend. It calmed and reassured Zachary, and having someone there as an advocate for him was so important. The police certainly jumped to conclusions seeing a young guy out at that time of night. They got started right away, asking Zachary questions and giving him sobriety tests. One was reciting the alphabet backward.

With the stress of the accident and still shaken physically, Zachary couldn't pass Z. Chris stepped right up, sharing that he had dyslexia and that the test was an unfair assessment. The questions continued until…*bam! Crash!* The tow truck driver had hit and finished off the other car.

Proving that he was not driving under the influence of any substances, the police officers' attention was focused now onto the tow truck driver.

Hours later, Zachary and Chris returned home, showing me pictures of the accident. My son sank into my arms, crying and whispering, "I love you, Mom." I was thankful to have my boy home safe and sound. To have Chris home, able to go and take care of our son, was something that I was extremely grateful for. He conducted himself calmly, determined, and effectively. I don't know what I would have done. I know I would never have been able to conduct myself in the same manner. Once again, my family was protected and safe. Thank you, Lord!

What Are the Chances?

With things not progressing positively regarding our battle with the bank, we had only fixed the house's bare necessities. At this point, this nightmare was approaching the ten-year milestone, and it was time to make a decision. With the legal battle not progressing and attorney bills mounting, we had to face the discouraging reality. The bank put us in a no-win situation with deep pockets and a legal team at the ready; we really had no other options. It didn't seem prudent to invest any more money in a home that would very likely be taken away from us.

In February, the heating system was struggling. One day it ultimately just stopped running. With temperatures still in the freezing zone, Chris directed Zachary to go to the local home improvement store to pick up electric heaters. They end up buying eight of them to put into each bedroom, one in the kitchen, and the rest in the basement to help keep the pipes warm so that they would not freeze. It ended up being one of those freezing periods in New England.

We bundled up in robes, stocking caps, and layers that kept us warm. The electric heaters and electric blankets were the extent of the heat in the house. We were grateful that the pipes didn't burst, but the cold mornings were harsh! Zachary tried to makeshift fix it, but nothing worked. His boss eventually found out about our dilemma and graciously had the crew come to our rescue and fix the burner. He said, "We take care of our own, and we consider you family." Smelling the heat from the baseboards that night was amazing! They had no idea how grateful we were!

The heating system was the tip of the iceberg. With each month came more and more issues with the house. The roof was leaking, windows and siding were not sealing correctly. The house was taking in water, which could only mean one thing: *mold*! We tried to keep the spaces that Chris was sleeping, eating, and spending his time as safe as possible during Chris's recovery, which means keeping it as clean and mold-free as much as we could.

Our court case, still lingering and being postponed, provided us with no direction. We needed to make a decision because the roof and its hazards were not safe for Chris. So our search for another place to reside started. So many things to consider. Should we rent an apartment and have the older kids stay with my parents? Should they remain in the house?

Each weekend we attended open houses and scanned the rental listings online and in the paper. Spring was still a couple of months away, and the market was not very good. We eventually found a place that was just remodeled and was being sold by an acquaintance. It was too small and wouldn't be big enough to house the whole family, but if we made some sacrifices, perhaps after some additions, we could make it work.

So we made some proposals to the owner. One was a short private mortgage; just enough time to get on our feet and see what would happen to our real home. The owners discussed it and made the decision that they couldn't do it. Knowing Chris's health situation, they were worried that if something happened to him—that if we were unable to make the payments—they would be forced to evict us, and they didn't want to be put into that predicament. Disappointed, but we understood. We kept trying to convince ourselves that it mustn't have been the one meant for us.

A month or so had passed; we were not close to finding a place that worked for our family, and that house had not yet sold. The asking price was coming down, and we were getting worried. Each month our attorney would say, "I have no idea what is going to happen. Things like this have never happened in the courts. We are on uncharted ground. I hope you have a place to go if things don't turn out as we would like." He was always supportive but realistic, and he was worried about Chris and his health needs and our family. So we continued to negotiate for the house, trying to convince ourselves that we could make it home. Finally, we had decided to make an offer on the house.

The night before we called the owner, Chris took my hands. He said, "Let's pray." We closed our eyes, and we prayed, asking that God would open the doors in the direction to where He (God) would like us to go and close the others. As we watched TV together, we received a text. It was from our friend who lived next door to us while we lived in the yellow colonial. Her text to us was, "You will never believe this, but the people who own the house you lived in are going to put the house back on the market. Can you believe it?" Now this friend had no idea that we were looking for other houses, let alone ready to put in an offer on another house the very next morning.

What are the chances that less than an hour after our prayer, we would receive the text? We immediately reached out to the owners and asked to meet with them. They responded to our text, and we met with them days later. What are the chances that we were meant to return to Hill Court, returning to that same yellow colonial? We were full of emotions: surprise, hope, confusion, elation, sadness. We had a chance to walk through the house, feeling at home and not at the same time.

After some negotiations, we agreed to terms and shook hands. So our family went from living on Mill Road to Hill Court, back to Mill Road, and now returning to Hill Court. It is astounding how much the Lord has protected and provided for us. Who are we to question or worry? If it is God's will, it will be done. Our family is truly blessed!

*****

Each day brought new challenges. Packing at the old house, moving back to the new house—where does everything go? We were once again downsizing, moving from a house twice the size of the new house. For many years, we added on to our home and filled every corner with everything a family may need, which made for a difficult transition. Two yard sales and still more left at the old house.

During the next few months of school and into the summer, everyone was stressed. Still not sure what was going on with the house on Mill, unable to let it go; it was our home. We built it to suit our family. The new house is beautiful. Everyone is impressed by it—the pool, the pool house, etc. We are grateful to have such a place to call home, but we miss our true home.

Any Questions?

So as usual, the summer flew by. One day I'm at my parents' house helping to deal with a situation. During my time there, Chris called and informed me that he needed to get to the ER ASAP. His ultrasound shows a blockage. He needs to get there now. So I quickly deal with my parents' circumstances and head home to bring Chris to the ER.

We end up being there from 5:00 p.m. to 12:00 a.m. in a holding pattern. The need to get there ASAP to begin treatment and tests seems not to have been communicated to the hospital staff. Miscommunication and bureaucracy make it a miserable place to be with Chris. He is not a very agreeable patient.

He was finally admitted at 1:00 a.m. No doctors to answer questions, procedures such as a catheter was used but unsure why, and we were discharged later that day with the discharge papers stating, "No hospital issues resolved." So we return home, I drop off Chris to rest, and I leave to go to my parents to address lingering issues with them left hanging from my quick departure the day before.

When I return home, I find a note requesting a call back to the imaging office that I went to a few days before for my yearly mammogram. I am informed that I need to go to another location for additional images and ultrasound. *Perfect! What now?* I quietly wonder. I anxiously await the date and go for the follow-up tests. I am told that I will get the results before I leave the office. Phew!

*****

So I patiently waited. The 3D mammograms are done first. Once the results are in, it will be determined if you need the ultrasound. I am told to remain in the waiting room. It felt like the air conditioning was off; I felt like I was quietly and secretly hyperventilating. I was sweating! Finally, the nurse came in. "Please follow me to the ultrasound room." My heart dropped! I lay there in the ultrasound room, staring up at beach scene posters.

I wish I could have been on one of those beaches at that moment. Wishing to be anywhere else for that matter. The technician completed the ultrasound and excused herself. Minutes later, she returns with a white-haired doctor who asks her to take additional images. He turns to me and explains that there are some concerning changes and growths that they would like to investigate further. He spoke very kindly and slowly to me, perhaps in an attempt to console me. He told me that I needed to go for a breast biopsy. He graciously asks if I have any questions. Questions? I have no idea what to ask; I just shake my head dismissively.

The technician quietly escorted me to the next nurse, who explained what was to be done during the biopsy and scheduled the procedure. I gathered my paperwork and emotions as I walked out to meet Chris patiently waiting for me in the car. We headed home, and during the ride, Chris kept me occupied with polite conversation about dinner plans and such. Thinking I am calm and ready, I share with him that the results didn't come back as hoped for and that I need to go for a biopsy, and I start to relay the information.

He asks questions: "When? Why? What does that mean?" Unable to articulate a sound, we end up sitting in the car, holding hands in silence for a while. That night, I find myself spiraling into a frenzy of worry. What if something is wrong? What if I get sick or worse? Who will take care of my family? What about work? I need to work for insurance. Chris needs his medication, and we can't afford it without insurance. What am I going to do?

The next couple of days were worrisome as I waited for the procedure, worrying about what the procedure entailed: *Was it painful? I'm terrified of needles!* Worrying about the results; did I want to know? The afternoon came, and it was time for the biopsy. Chris drove me and walked me in, reassuring me that he would be there waiting for me, and if I needed him that he would be in the waiting room.

I checked in, and after a short wait, my name was called. I walked with a chatty, friendly nurse. She informed me of what was going to happen, went over instructions on after the procedure care, and asked if I had any questions. Once again, I sat there numb. I had no questions; I wouldn't have known where to start. If it were Chris or the kids, I would have been the one with a notebook with prepared questions and jotting down responses. Instead I sat there on the hospital bed with my feet shaking and nervously swaying.

She takes me to another room to change and store my belongings in a locker. The johnnies are like cropped tops, mini versions of regular johnnies. I modestly tie the opening closed and wait in the room. An older woman is there, and she is nervously shaking her crossed legs. We watch the TV in an attempt to distract ourselves. As we wait, another patient returns to retrieve her belongings and informs her that she got good news and is free to go. She briefly gives her reassurance to the older lady that all will be good for her as well. She gets her clothes and gives me a comforting glance and nod.

Before I am picked up, a nurse enters and informs the older patient that she is all set. "You are free to go. Everything is okay, and no further tests are needed." As the nurse leaves, the lady looks at me and praises God in Spanish (or at least, I think she did, as she raises her hands and eyes toward heaven) and hurries to get her clothes and wishes me well. All of a sudden, my eyes well up, and I envy those two strangers. They were fine. But I was still here. I still had to do the biopsy!

Time for the biopsy. I was taken to the room and prepared. The nurse was a lovely lady. She went over the same information as the first nurse and continued with pleasantries. I stared up at the ceiling to posters of the beach once again. Boy, do I hate looking at those pictures! They aren't so comforting anymore. Maybe at the dentist or check-ups, but I am tired of seeing them now. The doctor came in, explaining again what was going to happen.

Once she was ready, she said the words I was dreading: "Take a deep breath." To my surprise, as she started, she pointed out that I could see what she was doing on the screen. When all was said and done, she looked at me and said, "All done, and boy, I can see that you are relieved." I guess I'm not as good at hiding my emotions. And yes, I was relieved.

More mammograms were required to be sure that the clip was inserted correctly. Once they were completed, I was able to leave. Now the waiting game. After a week, I started getting concerned: no calls. So I made calls to my doctor and the imaging office. I am told that the results were in days ago.

Now I am worried because they tell me that they will call my doctor's office, and I should hear back soon; no call for another day. Finally, on my way to work that next day, I got in touch with my doctor's office. The results were negative for cancer. I was fine! I took a deep breath, thanked God, and continued my drive to work.

My Golden Year!

The year 2020 came! I was turning fifty years old. In my mind, I still feel young, but the mirror tells me otherwise. My hair glittered with tinsel, as my student once so sweetly put it, forcing me to start considering coloring the gray away. Not wanting any celebration to ring in this golden year, an intimate party with just the five of us and my parents was planned. This disappoints my parents. They wanted to celebrate by taking the family to a fancy buffet at the casino in Connecticut because they knew how much I enjoyed the food.

However, Chris has been careful not to go into places with many people, restricting his errands due to his immunosuppressed status. Our family has incorporated behaviors such as taking off shoes as we enter the house, spraying our shoes and coats with Lysol spray, and using hand sanitizers often. It was my new *eau de parfum*. My family and friends joke and poke fun at me because of germophobic behavior, but I've always been one. Maybe a bit extreme, but it comforts me knowing that I am doing everything possible to keep Chris healthy.

So thoughtfully, Chris orders my favorite meal package: the Italian buffet from the local caterer—the one that catered our vow renewal ceremony. Even though it is a party for me, being the control freak that I am, I still have some influence and control. I ask that the items be picked up cold. It is during the time that people are sick with colds and the flu. There is mention of a new type of virus in the news, but not much is known about it; so better safe than sorry. Getting food and heating it to the right temperature should kill anything that would be dangerous to Chris.

The dinner and the evening spent with my family is just how I wanted to spend my birthday. Soleil and the boys decorate the house with golden balloons and a golden happy-birthday banner. A trip to

Italy stuffed in a card would have been nice too, but I was content with the Italian buffet. I was happy to spend my day with the ones most dear to me, opening gifts so carefully chosen, like a tote bag adorned by golden accents filled with all things gold—even a mini travel hand sanitizer with gold glitter. My mom could rival Martha Stuart in choosing gifts and planning parties. The dinner and gifts topped off with my favorite chocolate cake and white buttercream frosting; such a sweet ending.

At school, my teammates informed me that we would have a breakfast treat in honor of my birthday. I am fortunate to work with such supportive and wonderful friends. At 8:00 a.m., I am called to my friend's classroom under the guise that my help is needed. This is a tradition that we started many years ago, and one that we continue to follow. The birthday girl walks in to find the surprise birthday treats as we all sit down to enjoy a few moments together before starting our day with our students. However, an announcement rings across the school intercom. "There is an emergency meeting in the library in five minutes." Our breakfast would have to wait.

The principal and vice principal stand with grim faces; as the staff files into the library, they start to address those in attendance.

The principal informs us, "Following the dismissal bell at 3:30 p.m., the school will be closing due to the coronavirus." Teachers were directed to gather materials and supplies for students to take home with them and that not much information was available at the moment, but it will be shared as soon as possible.

A hum of questions and an uneasiness sweeps over the staff like a wave you aren't ready for at the beach. I will never forget the expressions on the faces of the staff. You could feel the sense of worry and fear in the group. The principal asks that we not panic; stay calm for the kids. It was our responsibility to remain calm and continue business as usual.

Help was offered to prepare and gather materials once we have determined what it would be. We were dismissed back to our rooms. Our heads, spinning and trying to comprehend what we just heard, gather our thoughts about what would be best to send home, and do it all while still teaching students. The bell rang, and students started arriving; time to plaster on the smile and greet and welcome the students.

That was how the pandemic, COVID-19, was introduced to my family and me. March was a horrifying month, watching the news station's broadcasts and learning all about this new virus and its deadly outcome. Not entirely sure as to how it spread and how to protect ourselves, schools, restaurants, and non-essential stores closed. People hoarded items like toilet paper, cleaning items, and hand sanitizer.

School ended up being remote for the rest of the year. It was strange to see my students only through a screen—long days of working on the Chromebook, answering texts, and calling student homes. The perception of many was that this time was a vacation for the teachers. The reality of it was that I was working harder and longer days during this year than I have over the past twenty-eight years of teaching, besides my first year of course. It was like I was a brand-new teacher learning all-new ways of teaching using new digital platforms, trying to learn how to navigate it myself, and help guide my students and their families.

Trying to balance the stress, long days of teaching, and the anxiety of the fear of someone in the family contracting the virus was too much to handle at times. Ending each night wiping down surfaces, countertops, doorways, and doorknobs became routine. Reminding everyone to wash their hands and not touch their face was overwhelming; nights of praying that we would all be safe, not only for us but particularly for Chris.

For a few months, Zachary continued to work as an HVAC assistant. Working and still being out in the workforce desensitized him to the fears that were built up in our house and our minds. Finding out that he met with some friends to show off his new vehicle nearly was the breaking point. Our house was a volcano ready to erupt.

Restrictions and guidelines were developed in our house. Zachary was asked to strip in the garage and shower immediately. During this time, we asked him to sleep in the basement and socially distance himself from Chris while it was meal times; otherwise, he wore a mask in the house to protect his father. The quarantine was not a punishment, and being banished to the finished basement with the futon and the large screen TV didn't turn out so bad.

Food shopping was an ordeal, one that I am grateful that the kids accepted to keep Chris and me from being exposed. "Pandemic shopping" was an adventure, geared up with their masks and a list in hand. Proteins were rationed, so the kids knew to look in other places like the frozen food aisle to find supplies. Upon arrival, bags were brought to the front door, and I was in charge of wiping down every item. Wiping the items, rinsing all the produce, was a feat in itself. While that was happening, the kids would strip and shower immediately.

Tensions mounted. If I reminded them about their masks or socially distancing one more time, I think they were ready to jump off a bridge. I couldn't help myself. The control freak and germophobic aspects of my personality were tearing me apart, resorting to sleeping in Zachary's bed while he was downstairs to not infect Chris—not that I had anything to infect him with.

With restrictions and closures, Zachary was informed of his employers' need to let him go which, at the time, we considered a blessing. It eased everyone's minds; now the five of us would be safe at home, and we could control where and when we would have to go out. It was a long spring. The five of us locked up in a small house was not ideal. Soleil and I teaching, and Samuel working on finishing eighth grade virtually made our daily life difficult. But we made it through.

The month of May came, and it was terrific and disappointing all at the same time. Due to the pandemic, all social gatherings of any kind were canceled. Unfortunately, that meant that Soleil would not be able to walk across the stage to accept her diploma. It was heartbreaking that after five years of hard work and determination, she would not be able to walk across the stage to receive the diploma that she worked so hard to obtain.

Feeling bad that she was not being recognized or celebrated in the way fitting her accomplishment, I decided to appeal to family and friends for help. Family members and friends made her posters and sent pictures of them to me. The creativity they all brought to the task was overwhelming! I then included the images in a book that I had printed so she is able to cherish this moment for years to come.

We surprised her on the day of her virtual graduation. Clapping and yelling while watching her picture appear on the Chromebook during her virtual commencement started off the festivities. Anyone who knows Soleil would not be surprised by her joking comments about enjoying her graduation ceremony much more from the comfort of her living room in her sweatpants.

As we gathered together as a family, the video her brother Zachary had been working on was revealed. The surprises continued. It consisted of short clips from family and friends wishing her luck on her new endeavors and congratulating her on all her accomplishments that they all have watched her achieve. Completing her student teaching virtually and not leaving the house for ten weeks, Chris and I felt it was imperative to plan a small gathering—within the social-distance guidelines of course.

Trying to keep the last surprise of the day a secret, I compiled a huge list of errands for Soleil to complete as we prepared for her graduation dinner. Little did she know what was in store! Her brothers helped decorate the front yard, maneuvering the trucks so she would not see the decorations. She questioned why I was requesting her to go get ready. She was wondering why I asked her to put a dress and makeup on. Again, anyone who knows Soleil can probably picture her sassy remarks to me, making such a request when she planned on staying in her quarantine outfit.

While she was getting ready, family, friends, and a few neighbors met in the front yard to honor the graduate and enjoy coffee and cupcakes. She was thoroughly surprised and overwhelmed by the gathering. Soleil is a wonderful mixture of sassy, spunky, and sensitive; with each surprise of the day, she became overwhelmed with tears, and of course, a witty comment always followed.

*****

The summer came with restrictions still in place. Thankful to be able to go outside now. This was a summer to help us appreciate the blessings that the Lord had bestowed on us. Not being able to go on day trips, have typical summer adventures, and not even being able to book the ferry and visit his sister in Long Island certainly was disappointing. However, how lucky we were to have such a beautiful pool and yard to enjoy. Sam was able to invite some of his friends over to have a campout. Each friend had their tent and was able to visit safely.

One day I walked out to the backyard to see Chris blowing up a floaty chair. I snapped. "Where did that come from?" I realized that he must have gone into a store to pick it up. He tried to reassure me that he safely picked it out in the store while they were preparing the chlorine order for the pool. My emotions got the best of me, and I had a screaming rant. "How could you? How can you be so stupid? You don't go anywhere. We do it all for you so you don't have to go anywhere. Is it all a joke?"

"No one is laughing. I was careful, and I did it for you," he responds with a look more deflated than the floaty he was trying to inflate for me. Realizing that he was trying to surprise me and do something for me, it was thoughtful, and I flipped out. Eventually, I was able to deescalate myself, and I apologized for the scene. Most of my summer days were spent floating in that inflatable chair, enjoying the pool, and quietly watching the clouds float across the sky.

Another unexpected outcome of quarantine was the food. Having time on her hands, Tik-Tok videos, and food channel episodes, Soleil blossomed as a chef. Dishes such as lo mein, homemade crab Rangoon, and taco casseroles were yummy distractions. Occasionally, finding the house in billowing clouds of smoke and discovering "medium-rare chicken" on the menu at the time was not comforting, but now is a joyful reminiscence.

Having a sous chef, whether novice or not, was a blessing. Afternoons of grilling hotdogs and dinners of chicken on the barbie gave our family a chance to bond poolside. Being restricted from shopping, placing orders for household items, and having them delivered to the house helped keep us safe and became a vital way to get what we needed.

The kids surprised us with the gift of a lifetime. They purchased a projector. Having a projector allowed us to have outdoor movies, which opened up a whole new world. Lighthearted evenings spent with my parents and having an opportunity to safely invite friends over to watch movies helped to ease the blow of quarantine.

Back to Normal?

Now, two years later, with the creation and distribution of COVID-19 vaccines and boosters, we pray for continued blessings and a hedge of protection. With restrictions, like mask mandates being lifted, we look forward to a return to some sense of normalcy. By no means do we expect or consider normalcy as synonymous to mundane. During the pandemic, our family faced challenges and gave thanks for our blessings. The isolation that our family experienced was no different than anyone else during this time; however, as restrictions were lifted, my anxiety and angst of giving my blessing allowing the children to slowly resume their social life was a source of contention. The children grew frustrated and yearned to have the ability to meet and spend time with their friends. I found it difficult to give a little leeway, and I dug my heels in. We had many arguments, resulting in tears and guilt. After some retrospection of the reasons I was demanding that they remain isolated and hearing Chris's feelings and his openness to allowing them to go out, I eventually conceded.

With the promise of mask wearing, social distancing as much as possible, and choosing venues that were less crowded, how could I deny them a chance to reconnect with their friends? They graciously put up with my reminders to keep safe and to use all the safety precautions that have managed to keep us healthy thus far. I work hard to end the goodbyes with a "*Have fun and I Love you*," to disguise my apprehension. The efforts of our family have been commendable and have been effective as we try to resume venturing back out into society. The family has been working hard, pulling together to assist each other, and acknowledging that the Lord is walking with us and supporting us. Samuel now in high school has grown into a confident adolescent. He has established himself as a competent, hardworking student while working with his peers and meeting his teachers' expectations—still easy going but driven to succeed and learn. As a student in the engineering shop, he has found an interest and a gift in learning and completing challenging projects. His father and I are so proud of him and anxiously await to see what direction the Lord takes him in his education and his future.

One blessing that was bestowed on me was a change in my position at the school. Due to a retirement, there was a posting for an academic coach. This position would take me out of the classroom and require me to assist teachers and the staff in various aspects of teaching and learning. Years ago, I had enrolled in a school leadership program with aspirations of perhaps taking the leap into administration. My graduate work earned me a master's degree in curriculum and instruction, which would be extremely useful as an administrator. However, that was also the same time period that I was blessed with Samuel. The news of being pregnant again signaled that it was not the time to start something new, so I remained in the classroom.

However, recognizing that there is no time like the present, it was scary to leave the classroom, but I decided to throw my hat into the ring. I interviewed for the position and was blessed with the appointment. Leaving the classroom and the position I've maintained for the last twenty-eight years was bittersweet. Questioning whether I made the right decision resulted in many sleepless nights. This new position involved new responsibilities, and I have so much to learn. Being in the classroom for so long, I knew what to expect, I enjoyed being part of a grade level team, and I also enjoyed working with my students. But as time passes, I am learning my way and have found that I enjoy collaborating with and supporting teachers as they hone their skills in being effective educators.

Both Soleil and Zachary have been blessed with new jobs as well during this time. Soleil interviewed and was appointed to a teaching position at my school! I know, you are probably thinking that she moved forward because of me. I wish I could say that I had that much clout in the school, but I don't and I also removed myself completely from the interviewing process, which was difficult for me. I am proud to say that she earned her position all on her own merit.

She applied and interviewed with the hiring committee. After the initial interview, she and a few other candidates were moved forward and asked to present a lesson in a class for the committee. I can't even convey my excitement when I received a text from her while I was in a meeting that read, "I got it! I was offered a job as a fourth grade teacher!" Such a proud moment to be able to introduce her to the staff as the newest hire. Having the opportunity to work with her now on a daily basis is a chance of a lifetime. Watching her grow into a competent, effective educator truly completes me as a mom and as an academic coach.

Zachary, as well, has been blessed to find employment, which he is happy to say is "a gift from God." During the pandemic, he was laid off from his HVAC job. When businesses started to reopen, it was necessary for him to start looking for a new job. He interviewed for a number of positions virtually, which was not his forte. He was getting discouraged and eventually secured a third shift job with a large online retail company. Adjusting to the late-night shifts, sleeping during the day, and not seeing the family because he worked on the weekends definitely had an effect on him both physically and emotionally. With the promise to continue to search for an HVAC job, we supported him to quit and accept a seasonal laborer position. Many days, he would drag himself into the house, covered with cement and exhausted from the hard work. Nonetheless, he kept his promise of sending out resumes and applying for jobs. One day, he received a call from a company that he had previously applied to following his high school graduation. He did not get the job then, but after a phone and an in-person interview, he was offered employment! It is so rewarding to watch him now eagerly prepare and proudly leave each morning to start his day. Now he takes pride in himself, feels like part of a team, and feels appreciated by his employer. We all thank God for this blessing as we recollect those days of dragging him out of bed to go to school and those trying times of insecurity and self-doubt.

*****

Winter managed to bring a number of snowstorms to New England leaving a wintry mess to be cleaned up. It was the beginning of February, and vacation was a couple of weeks away. After a long work week, I was looking forward to some rest and relaxation during the weekend. I was hoping to regroup and prayed for strength to help me make it through until vacation. Unfortunately, Saturday started off very stressful for the family. The cars were covered with snow, the house demanded its usual cleaning needs and responsibilities such as laundry and food shopping made family interactions and conversations tense.

In an attempt to escape the tension, Chris decided to feverishly clean the snow off of the cars. He entered the house to take a break, sitting at the kitchen table to catch his breath. This was not unusual behavior because Chris frequently attempts to complete tasks quicker than his body is able. Frustrated that my hopes to relax seemed to be melting away as quickly and as surely as the delicate snowflakes were doing outside. I continued my housekeeping, paying no attention to him. While I was vacuuming, Chris shared with Soleil that he didn't feel quite right. Since I was so focused on trying to get the work done and being upset that Chris was not helping, I brushed off Soleil's pleas to attend to her father. I angrily dismissed her when she said, "Mom, Dad said he doesn't feel so well, and I don't think he looks so good." Utilizing her lifeguarding background, she became increasingly concerned by his excessive yawning.

I continued to do my chores until Soleil demanded that I check on her father. So I conceded and headed to the kitchen, finding him slumped over the table. Still convinced that he was fine, I suggested we call our friend and neighbor to come over and check his vitals. Minutes later, she arrived. She took his pulse, listened to his heart, and asked him some questions. It was her suggestion that we take him to the urgent care that she worked at because he was now complaining of chest pressure and radiating pain to his shoulder. Gratefully, she drove ahead to talk and update the doctor of Chris and his health needs and concerns. As Soleil and Zachary arrive, they are informed that the doctor advised going straight to the hospital since it was Saturday and there wasn't any way to do the needed bloodwork.

Since the urgent care was just down the street, they were back home in no time. Stubborn Chris sat on the couch, refusing to go to the hospital. *No, I just need to lay down. I just need to catch my breath.* As he laid there, color drained from his face, and we decided that we needed to call the ambulance. The rescue arrived in what seemed to be a few seconds. The Emergency Medical Technicians (EMTs) filed into the house, carrying boxes of equipment asking questions about his current health concerns, symptoms, medications, and allergies. As they asked the questions, they quickly and efficiently inserted an IV and placed wires and stickers all over his chest. An electrocardiogram (EKG) was performed, and they identified that Chris was having a heart issue. He was moved to a chair, and they carried him outside to an awaiting gurney. Carefully, he was shuffled onto the gurney and into the rescue. The EMT reassured us that they had everything in the ambulance needed to help Chris and that they would get him there as quickly as possible. Following evaluation, it was confirmed that he had suffered a heart attack, two blockages were identified and surgery was imperative. Less than an hour later, Chris was in the "cath lab," which was the surgical room where the procedure of inserting a cardiac catheter would be performed.

No visitors allowed in the hospital due to COVID numbers compounded the stress and worry. Eventually, the cardiac surgeon called and informed us that the surgery was successful. Two stents later, the blockages were removed; he was moved to the Cardiac Intensive Care Unit for observation. Amazingly, he was awake and coherent later that night. After three days, he was discharged. The doctor conferenced and shared with us that "he received the needed intervention at the exact best time. If you would have waited, things could have been a lot worse! His prognosis is good." I am so thankful that Soleil was there and attentive to notice that things were not right. Following the recent events, it is my belief once again that Chris is being protected by the Lord and his guardian angel!

Sunset

Who would have imagined that after all we have encountered and overcame that we would still be together twenty-eight-plus years later? It has not been an easy road, but we are still here together, facing each day together. Through the good and the bad, sickness and in health, we have stood by our pledge to each other and God. With the Lord's assistance and glory, Chris has been sober for more than eighteen years now. We pray that our storms and difficult trials are behind us. Certainly, we still have our days; but more than not, I continue to find myself giggling at his silly jokes, enjoying the view of the ocean, and treasuring the feeling of my toes in the warm sand, holding hands with Chris.

Knowing how high the divorce rate is, you may question how we have remained together. Who would have imagined battling the bank, emotionally dealing with each medical emergency, and struggling to hold onto a marriage through tumultuous times? But also such a miracle: acknowledging the blessings, like having medically trained neighbors when Chris was in need; or to be able to smile or just breathe during a difficult time; having a total stranger be inspired to be Chris's donor; and experiencing wonderful times—such as our children's births, proms, and graduations—which are all part of our story. All due to the intervention of our Heavenly Father.

After each season in our lives, we acknowledge the presence and the protection of God. We are thankful for all our blessings and are especially thankful for our children who all have faith and are growing into people we are proud of. We have attributed our determination and strength to overcome adversity as a gift of God.

I remember sitting in the hospital with Chris during a worrisome time of his transplant recovery, spending the day wearily watching reruns of the same TV shows that we watched during Chris's previous hospitalization. Unexpectedly, we heard a knock on the door, and an individual asks if she can come in. She introduced herself as the chaplain, sharing that she was visiting patients to offer consult. She asked how things were going and listened intently to Chris's recount of his blessings and woes, nodding her head—indicating that she was listening and validating him.

Before she left, she asked if she could share some advice. She did not read from a script or journal, but her words ring true to this day: "There are three things to remember: *Life*. Treasure the life you are living. Live each day as best as you can. *Love*. Love deeply and completely. And finally, *let go*. Let go of the things that are of no worth to you, that are holding you back, which we understand as forgiveness."

I'm not sure where she heard that or if she made it up herself, but it was just what we needed at the time; and I hope it helps you at a time of need. Holding on to hurt and disappointment holds you back from living and loving. Life is too short to not move on and acknowledge the blessings that you have been granted. So my final suggestion to you is to take a deep breath, carry on, and don't be discouraged; you are always welcome to walk a day in my flip-flops! May God bless you!

About the Author

Rita Marcotte is a dedicated wife and mother of three beautiful children. Responding to the call to be an educator, she completed her studies and is a first-generation college graduate. After teaching in an elementary school setting as a second-grade teacher for nearly thirty years, Rita embarked on a new journey, changing her role from teacher to academic coach to share her knowledge with a new generation of teachers.

Besides being a wife and mother, she has worn many hats, including camp counselor, Girl Scout troop leader, baseball coach, Alpha Delta Kappa member, and CCD teacher. Above all, she is a devout daughter of the Lord. Her faith has carried her through all of life's endeavors, remaining humble and optimistic through it all. She is an example of grace and poise for her loved ones and for all who know her.